Dad's GREAT ADVICE FOR TEENS

Great Advice Books also available at greatadvicegroup.com

Great Advice for Everyone

Great Advice for College Students

Great Advice for New Drivers

Upcoming Great Advice Books

Great Advice for Dating

Great Advice for Young Kids

Great Advice for Graduates

Great Advice for Job Seekers

Great Advice for Newlyweds

Great Advice for Expectant Parents

Great Advice for New Parents

Great Advice for Parents of Toddlers

Dad's GREAT ADVICE FOR Teens

MARC FIENBERG

For my four teens and almost-teens,

and the woman who gave them to me.

CONTENTS

BONUS ADVICE

Do You Really Need to Read This Book?

There are two types of people in this world: those who are perfect and happy, and those who have some small problems in their lives and aren't quite as happy as they could be.

If you're perfect, and your social life, your school life, your relationship with your parents, your friends, and your family are all, well, perfect, and you're already as happy as you can be, then you definitely should not waste your time reading this book.

But if you're not perfect—if you have problems; if you have issues you're dealing with; if you question yourself; if you lack self-confidence; if you're anxious; if you procrastinate; if you're always trying to make others happy; if you worry about sex, drinking, smoking, vaping, or drugs; if you're looking for balance in your life; if you're afraid to become the person who you were meant to be; or if you're just not as happy as you want to be, then maybe this book can help you.

Since the day you were born, your parents have tried to teach you as much as they could to prepare you for your life as an adult, and have gone out of their way to make you as happy as possible. But as a teen, you're becoming much more independent and responsible for your own decisions and actions. And as you get older, the decisions you're going to have to make, and the problems and issues you'll face, are only going to get bigger and more important. Even though your parents will likely always be there to help you through your problems and advise you with important decisions, as a teen,

I'm sure you also want to become independent by solving your problems and making smart decisions on your own.

And that's the purpose of this book: To help you start to take more responsibility and control of your life and decisions, and ultimately, to help you get happy. You'll notice I said "get happy" rather than "be happy." I phrased it that way to emphasize that happiness is not something you can just automatically "be," but rather, it's something you have to work for and go "get."

If you're interested in doing a little work for it and getting happy, then I've got some good advice for you. In fact, dare I say, I've actually got some Great Advice for you. And this Great Advice has been rigorously tested day after day for many years... by my own children. I have four kids, two of whom are teens and two of whom are about to become teens. And as you might expect, my kids have had some of the very same problems and issues and thoughts and feelings over the years that you may now have as a teen. After a lot of deep, meaningful discussions, I've been fortunate to be able to give them Great Advice to help them make important decisions and solve problems in their lives.

Usually, when I passed along Great Advice to my kids, it was in a one-on-one, private conversation. But I often wanted to share that Great Advice with my other children. The problem, however, was that some of my kids weren't old enough to really hear that advice yet. And so...

I started to write down the Great Advice, without my kids ever knowing. Every night, before I went to sleep, I'd secretly write another piece of Great Advice. Very soon, I had built up quite a repertoire. When my eldest daughter turned thirteen, I bound up all the advice into a book as a birthday present for her. It was called *Great Advice from Your Father*. When my second oldest daughter turned thirteen, I did the same thing, and I'll do it again when my other daughter and son each turn thirteen.

Those books were the genesis for the book you're now holding. And just like it helped my own kids, the Great Advice I'll offer you can help you:

- Build your confidence
- Be productive with your time
- Develop close relationships
- Make good decisions
- Take smart risks
- Follow your passion
- Take action toward your goals
- Create new, positive habits
- Stay positive when problems arise
- Make a difference in the world

Once you've finished reading *Dad's Great Advice for Teens*, I hope that, not only will you agree that the title fits, but you'll feel like this book has helped you, changed you, improved your life, and most of all, helped you get happier than you were when you started reading it. If you're like most of the teens that have read this book before you, it most certainly will.

But obviously, you can read this Great Advice if you want to, or not. You can take it to heart if you want to, or not. You can put it into action if you want to, or not. What you do with this Great Advice is up to you. But I want to make sure you have access to this Great Advice for two main reasons:

Because these are important things to know about, to think about, and to do, and thus will make you a happier person.

And because I really want you to "get happy."

Enjoy the book,

Marc

.

Wait! Before You Begin…

Before you dive in and start reading, I want to make sure you know how to squeeze every ounce of value you possibly can out of this book. Of course, you're welcome to simply just read this book, and I know you'll get a lot out of it by doing so. But reading it is really just the first step. Reading Great Advice isn't all that that valuable if you don't take action afterward. You need to do more than just read it. You need to live it.

If you need an extra little "nudge" to do that, I developed a short checklist of a few simple challenges that will help you put the Great Advice into effect. Think of this "Challenge Checklist" as a companion to this book. For each piece of Great Advice you read, I've included some simple tasks you can do to immediately see the benefits of putting the Great Advice to work for you. Some of the challenges are difficult, some are easier, some are scary, and some are simply thought-provoking. You can do each challenge after reading each piece of Great Advice, or you can pick and choose the ones that resonate with you the most. Heck, even if you don't read the book at all, you can STILL check off some challenges and get something really valuable out of the checklist.

So come on, challenge yourself!! I'll email you the "Challenge Checklist" right now if you go to:

greatadvicegroup.com/checklist2

DON'T DO REALLY DUMB THINGS

Before you do anything really dumb, ask yourself if you're willing to live with the worst-case scenario.

There's this friend of mine who, as a teenager, did some dumb things. (Not me, I swear, just my friend.) His name is... Archimedes Clutterbuck. He did some dumb things that we don't necessarily have to go into right now, but let's just say that those things were... dumb.

However, even though my friend Archimedes (again, not me) did some dumb things, he was fortunate enough that he didn't do any Really Dumb Things.

Scientists recently discovered that 94 percent of teenagers have a specific gene, which they've named the RDT gene, that genetically predisposes them to do Really Dumb Things. There's a 96 percent chance that that's not actually true and I just made up the whole thing, but regardless, I believe the discovery is inevitable someday soon.

Why?

Admittedly, people of all ages are guilty of doing some Really Dumb Things, but teenagers seem to do their disproportionate share of them. Just look at YouTube if you want to see lots of examples of teenagers challenging each other to swallow spoonfuls of cinnamon, light themselves on fire, hop out of moving cars, and eat laundry detergent pods. Yum!

There's a huge difference between doing dumb things and Really Dumb Things. A dumb thing is something that will get you grounded. A Really Dumb Thing is something that will get you thrown in jail. A dumb thing is something silly you do that your friends discover and tease you about for a few days. A Really Dumb Thing is something shameful you do that goes viral for which the entire internet trolls you for several years. A dumb thing is something that earns you a trip to the doctor's office. A Really Dumb Thing is something that gets you a trip to the emergency room.

So how do you figure out the difference between a dumb thing and a Really Dumb Thing?

It's simple. Ask yourself just two questions. The first question is, "What are the chances that this potentially Really Dumb Thing will go badly?" Or said differently, "What are the chances that I'll get caught, I'll get injured, or that the Really Dumb Thing will be made public?" Spend a few moments to give yourself an honest, analytical assessment of the chances that things won't go well. Once you've done this... totally ignore your answer, because aside from the fact that you are going to significantly underestimate the probability of something going wrong, the answer to that question doesn't really matter.

The real question that matters is the second one.

And that question is, "On the small chance that the Really Dumb Thing I'm about to do actually goes bad, *can I live with the consequences?*" Assume for a moment that the worst-case scenario actually happens, and you do get caught, or injured, or discovered, and then visualize what your life will look like afterward. If that visualization includes prison bars, or a wheelchair, or a news story about you that goes viral for the wrong reasons, that's a good sign that maybe you shouldn't do the Really Dumb Thing.

On the other hand, if the consequences of doing the Really Dumb Thing are bad, but it's something you can live with, something for which the results will only linger for a matter of minutes, hours, or days, then go ahead and take your chances if you think it's worth it. (Hint: it probably isn't.)

Here's a good example of the difference between a dumb thing and a Really Dumb Thing. Let's say you're thinking about drinking beer while you're underage. What happens if you get caught? Well, in this day and age, it probably means a misdemeanor ticket and some community service—certainly not something you'd want, but also probably not something that's going to follow you around the rest of your life.

Contrast that with the consequences of getting caught drinking and driving. Even if you avoid the worst-case scenario of you accidentally killing another human being, getting caught most likely means an arrest, a mugshot, an overnight stay in jail, your parents paying money to bail you out, an expensive lawyer, a trial, and perhaps even a felony conviction with some prison time. Even if you think you can survive prison or juvenile detention for a few months (you can't), a felony conviction is one of those things that really does follow you around for the rest of your life. Every time you apply for a job they'll ask if you've ever had a felony conviction, and every time they ask you, you'll have to tell them about the Really Dumb Thing you did one night ten, twenty, or thirty years ago. Heck, even the best-case scenario, in which you only lose your driver's license, is still pretty darn bad.

Even if you believe you're the smartest, cleverest, most cunning drunk driver in the world who takes extra precautions not to get caught, is it worth that small chance that you actually will get caught, and you'll be a felon the rest of your life, or lose your driver's license? I don't know about you, but the answer for me is "no." And if you're smart, or just not Really Dumb, the answer for you will be "no" too.

Here's another way to think about it. If I gave you a gun with one hundred chambers in it and only one bullet, and I offered you ten million dollars to point it at your head and pull the trigger, would you do it? Even though the chances of something bad happening are just 1 percent, the consequence of something bad happening is your death. Could you accept the 1 percent chance that you might die? I hope that your answer is "no." And if your answer is indeed "no," you should use this same example when presented with the choice of doing a Really Dumb Thing.

By all means, take chances and do risky things in life. Risky things are what make life fun and exciting. Just make sure that you can tell the difference between taking a risk on a smart thing, a dumb thing, and most importantly, a Really Dumb Thing.

Be sure you can tell the difference between a risk for which you can live with the consequences and a risk for which the consequences would be really, really, really, bad. Because that would qualify as a Really Dumb Thing. And you don't want to do Really Dumb Things.

#reallydumbthings

#dontdoreallydumbthings

"If you don't want anyone to find out, don't do it."

–Chinese Proverb

DON'T MAKE YOUR PARENTS HAPPY

Be your own person, and make yourself happy, not your parents, because all they want is for you to be happy anyway.

As humans, we look to other people for approval and validation sometimes. You probably look to your friends, teachers, social media followers, and others to see how "cool" your clothes, jokes, friends, hair, grades, makeup, shoes, and other things are. (Your hair looks great, by the way. I love what you've done with it!)

If you've ever posted anything to Instagram and checked every three minutes for the next twelve hours to see how many "likes" you received, then you know what I'm talking about. But if you're like most teens, of all the people you're looking to for approval, on the very top of that list is... your parents.

Teenagers are known for going out of their way to drive their parents crazy. After all, that's really your primary job as a teen, right? Ironically, you probably also spend a lot of energy trying to make your parents happy and proud of you.

You should know though, teens who expend a lot of effort to make their parents happy and proud of them turn into adults who expend a lot of effort to make their parents happy and proud of them. And a lot of those adults spend a large portion of their lives, sometimes their entire lives, continuing to expend a lot of effort to make their parents proud of them, sometimes even after their parents are dead and gone. (And trust me, it's not easy to make somebody proud once they're dead.)

The industry for psychologists and therapists is about 20 billion dollars, and in my very unscientific estimate, about 19.6 billion of that is driven by people looking for help with issues in getting their parents' approval. And if you were to interview all the doctors and lawyers in the world, I'm pretty sure you'd find that about 34.8 percent of them became doctors or lawyers because their parents wanted them to.

Don't fall into this trap. Don't spend your life trying to gain the approval of your parents, or of anybody else in this world. It's hard enough to figure out what it is that YOU want out of life, and then accomplish it, let alone try to temper that with what your parents want. And it's a sure recipe for unhappiness.

My good friend Archimedes Clutterbuck wanted to be a doctor when he was in high school. Or to be more accurate, his parents wanted him to be a doctor. "But Archie," I said, "every time you give blood, you faint." Regardless, he spent four years getting a pre-med degree, then four years in medical school, then five years as a resident, and then he officially became a doctor. And when he stood up on that stage as they handed him his medical license, he looked out at his parents in the audience, smiles plastered across their faces, beaming with pride. His parents took him out to a celebratory dinner, bought him a fancy dessert, gave him a fancy stethoscope as a gift, and then... they went home. And Archimedes was left standing there... as a doctor. Going to work... as a doctor. Being... a doctor. Every day. For the rest of his life. (Fortunately, Archie soon quit his job as a doctor, and was ten times happier as a result.)

Now put yourself in Archie's shoes. Imagine you don't really want to be a doctor, but you spent thirteen years studying to be a doctor just to make your parents proud. Imagine that you have a lifetime ahead of you, doing something every day that you don't really want to do. Imagine that every day of your life, you'll be making your parents really happy, but not yourself. And chances are, if you're like most people who find themselves in this situation, you'll become more and more miserable day after day, week after week, month after month, year after year. But on the plus side, at least your parents will be happy, right?

Wrong.

You probably won't ever really believe this until you have children of your own, but most parents are proud of their kid regardless of what their kid does or accomplishes in life. Nothing you can do can decrease—or for that matter, increase—the amount of pride your parents have in the person that you are. Nothing you can do can increase or decrease the amount of love your parents have for you. Your parents' pride and love for you is unconditional and infinite. (If you want to prove the point, go ahead and smash grandma's antique vase and see if your parents get over it. Hint: They will. Eventually.)

When you succeed at something, that smile on your parent's face is not a look of pride; it's happiness at the pride that you probably feel about yourself. When you fail at something, that sad look on your parent's face is not a look of shame; it's sadness at the disappointment that you might feel about yourself. And strangely, sometimes when you fail at something, you might be observant enough to see a tiny gleam of a smile on your parent's face. Trust me, it's not your parent secretly experiencing a bit of schadenfreude at your failure. It's their happiness that you risked failure, and had the strength to give it your best.

In the end, your parents really only want one thing for you: happiness.

Are there exceptions to this parenting rule? Of course. A lot in fact. Many parents screw up royally. They push you in a direction that they think will make YOU happy, even though they don't realize that they're actually pushing you in a direction that will make THEM happy. Don't tell your parents I revealed this closely guarded secret, but as it turns out, many parents actually make mistakes. And this parenting mistake might even be one of the more common ones. But your job is to make sure you don't let their mistake become yours.

Regardless of what your parents want for you under the guise of making you happy, only you know what's really going to make yourself happy. Whatever that thing is, do that. Wholeheartedly. With no apologies. And no matter how hard it is for your parents in the short term, remind yourself that, in the end, if you're happy with your decision, your parents will probably realize that they're happy too. And if you're in the unfortunate situation of having parents that don't ever get to that place of happiness, it ends up being their problem, not yours.

Make sure that the path you choose in life is one you choose for your own reasons, to make yourself proud and happy, not to impress your parents, or to gain your parents' approval.

#makeyouhappy

#pleaseyourself

#dontpleaseyourparents

"It's important to make somebody happy, and it's important to start with yourself."

–Unknown

SPEND YOUR 44 HOURS WISELY

Spend your free time on the things that will bring you lasting happiness, not just things that are fun in the moment.

"I don't have time for that."

I hear it all the time, from teens and adults alike. But *really?* You don't have time for "that," whatever "that" is?

Allow me to convince you otherwise.

I'm not great at math, but with 24 hours in a day, and 7 days in a week, that gives you 168 hours to spend as you please every single week of every single month of every single year of your life. This is true regardless of your race, religion, sexual orientation, where you live, how much money you have, what country you come from, how smart you are, how pretty you are, or how nice you may be. Time is the great equalizer; we are all given the same amount of time each week no matter what our lot is in life.

Sadly, if you're one of those human beings that need to sleep every night, then you lose a bunch of those 168 hours. But even after accounting for eight hours of sleep a night (if you're lucky), that leaves you with 112 hours each week.

"But school!" you say. "What about school?"

Even after accounting for eight hours of school every weekday, that leaves you with 72 hours each week.

"Yeah, but I've got homework. Soccer practice. Lots of chores. And my memes! I love memes! I gotta have time to look at my memes!"

Even after accounting for four hours a day of some mandatory obligations you have to take care of, and of course, those all-important memes, that leaves 44 hours each week.

And 44 hours every week is A LOT of time.

All of this makes the statement, "I don't have time for that," a little hard to believe. While you have the physical need to sleep, and an obligation to go to school and do homework, you have control over how you prioritize and spend those remaining 44 hours in your week. So rather than saying, "I don't have time for that," a better, more accurate statement would be, "I don't want to spend my time doing that." That at least acknowledges that you have control over how you prioritize spending your 44 hours. And once you realize that you do have control over how you spend your 44 hours, make sure you spend them wisely.

Keep track of how you're spending your 44 hours, because what you'll find is that, day by day, week by week, year by year, those hours will slip away from you.

You'll spend those hours on things that are easy to spend them on, the most common one being consuming television, videos, or social media. It's relaxing. It's enjoyable. And it's easy, so why not? You deserve some downtime, don't you?

You do! But keep track of how much downtime you give yourself. The average teenager spends about three hours watching television each day. That brings your 44 hours down to 23. And the average teenager also spends about three hours on social media each day. Sadly, that leaves you with just two measly hours each week.

So how are you supposed to spend your 44 hours? How are you supposed to think about your 44? It's not easy, but I've found that the best way to think about how you want to spend your 44 hours is by separating them into two main categories: "Today Me" hours and "Tomorrow Me" hours.

Today Me hours are hours you spend making yourself happy now—relaxing or enjoying the moment, giving you instant short-term gratification. They are hours spent on things like watching videos, consuming social media, napping, and of course, looking at memes!

Tomorrow Me hours are hours you spend that might not be quite as relaxing or enjoyable in the moment (although they can be), but that will make you happy over the long term, for weeks, months, years, or a lifetime. They are hours you spend doing things like studying for an algebra test, practicing the guitar, or learning how to create your own memes!

Today Me hours make Today Me pretty darn happy, but kind of upset Tomorrow Me, who never really gets to enjoy those hours. Tomorrow Me hours frustrate Today Me, who could be having a much better time, but make lots of Tomorrow Me's happy.

There's room for both types of hours in your day—things you do just to enjoy the moment and recharge your batteries, and things you do that are a bit of an investment for future enjoyment. It's obviously very easy to spend your Today Me hours, but a bit more effort and discipline is required to spend Tomorrow Me hours. If you need help motivating yourself to spend Tomorrow Me hours, just try to remind Today Me that, even though they might not be so happy right now, Tomorrow Me is going to be really grateful and happy for the Tomorrow Me hours you're spending today.

Keep track of how many of your 44 you are spending on Today Me hours, watching something, looking at someone else's creations, relaxing, bringing yourself instant gratification and enjoyment, but no meaningful benefit once the television show or YouTube video is over. And keep track of how many of your 44 you are spending on Tomorrow Me hours, helping you learn something, create something, connect with somebody, reach your goals, become a better person, or assist somebody else in becoming a better person.

Forty-four hours a week, every week of the year, every year of your life, leaves you LOTS of time outside of sleep, school, and homework to do other things. Use that time wisely, on things that will bring you lasting happiness, and even though Today Me won't have quite as much fun, Tomorrow Me will thank you.

#spendyour44wisely

#whatwillyoudowithyour44

#44everyweek

"The chief cause of failure and unhappiness is trading what you want most for what you want right now."

–Zig Ziglar

DON'T BELIEVE A WORD YOUR BOYFRIEND/GIRLFRIEND SAYS

When trying to figure out how "into you" your boyfriend/girlfriend is, put more weight on what they do, than what they say.

There are many honest people in this world who say exactly what they mean and, for better or worse, will truly express how they feel about their significant other. The world needs as many of these people as possible.

And yet, there are others who are not so honest and forthright— people who are, to use a technical term, jerks.

There's a well-known stereotype out there about the male gender that goes something like this: "Guys only have one thing on their minds." Naturally, that one thing is... Taco Bell.

OK, it's *not* Taco Bell. The one thing they're referring to on every guy's mind is... sex (or any kind of sexual experience), although Taco Bell might run a close second.

Like all stereotypes, it's unfair to apply this to everyone. There are a lot of guys out there who don't have a one-track mind. And conversely, there are a lot of girls who, like some guys, only have that same thing on their minds too.

Whether a guy or a girl, having sex in their thoughts isn't, in itself, a bad thing. Every single one of the 7.8 billion people on this planet owe their existence to sex, and almost every single one of those 7.8 billion people will have some sort of sexual experience before they leave this planet. And because there are approximately 7.8 billion people having sex, whoever invented sex way back when made sure that it was a fun, enjoyable experience.

The fact that many guys and girls often seem to have sex on their mind isn't the problem. The real problem is that when sex is the only thing on somebody's mind, a person tends to say anything they need to say to convince somebody else to satisfy that amazingly strong human desire, whether it's true or not. They might say things like, "I love you so much," or "I want to be in a committed relationship and only date you," or "I really care a lot about you," when it doesn't really reflect their true feelings.

Now some people really mean it when they say those things. But some don't. So how do you know which type of person you're talking to? How can you tell the person that really means the beautiful things they say, from the person that doesn't? How can you tell the person who really cares about you from the person who really only cares about fooling around with you?

It's actually quite simple: *Don't listen to what they say; watch what they do.*

Here are some things that people DO that demonstrate they might not like you as much as you think they do:

- They say they're going to do something with you, but then cancel or don't follow through.
- They always have to have things their way, rarely giving in or compromising.
- They ask for lots of favors, but don't do many favors for you.
- They only make plans with you at the last minute, when they don't have anything else to do.

- They disrespect you by saying mean things or calling you names.
- They don't call or text you that often.
- They don't ask questions about you.
- They don't take interest in the things you're interested in.
- They don't introduce you to their friends, or don't pay attention to you when their friends are around.
- They often can't find time to be with you because they're too busy.

On the other hand, here are some things that people DO that demonstrate that they probably really like you:

- They do the things they say they're going to do.
- They often give in and compromise.
- They do favors for you when you ask.
- They make plans with you days or weeks in advance.
- They say nice things to you, and say nice things about you.
- They call and text you often.
- They ask a lot of questions about you, and about what's going on in your life.
- They take interest in the things you're interested in, even if those things don't interest them.
- They introduce you to their friends, and pay close attention to you when their friends are around.
- They try to spend a lot of time with you, even if they're busy.
- They try to do things that make you happy, and try to avoid doing things that make you unhappy.

You'll notice a common theme among most of the items above: They all take a lot of time.

Somebody that really cares about you wants to spend time with you, and wants to spend time doing things that make you happy. Somebody that doesn't really care about you, has an easy time saying nice things (which doesn't take that much time), but has difficulty spending the time that it takes to demonstrate that they really care about you.

In short, a jerk will say anything they can to get what they want, because it's quick and easy to fake. But they won't usually DO the things that show they care, because it takes a lot more time to fake that.

If you're questioning somebody's feelings for you, ignore all the things they say, and pay attention to all the things they do.

#watchdontlisten

#dodontsay

#actionsspeaklouder

#qualitytime

"Actions speak louder than words."

–Proverb

BE CONTRADISTINCTIVE

Don't be afraid to be different. Be yourself and be proud of your unique differences.

Most teenagers just want to fit in. They want to be like their friends, their teachers, their parents, their role models. And that's just fine... if that's who you are.

But without the pressure of trying to fit in and be accepted by your peers, you might just decide to be a bit *contradistinctive*. (That's just a fancy word for "different," because I was trying to be a bit... contradistinctive.)

How do I know? Because deep down inside, most of us are contradistinctive in some unique way.

It's a nice platitude to say you are a unique individual, but in a very scientific way, it's true. Each of us has our own unique DNA, a unique combination of 6.4 billion nucleotides that has never before been seen in the history of the universe. In fact, even if you have an identical twin, your DNA is still not exactly the same as your twin's. And that unique, never before seen DNA, in large part, is what makes you *you*.

Even though each one of us is different, you probably try very hard not to appear different. You probably try very hard to fit into your group of friends, to be like them, act like them, do the things

31

that they do, and say the things that they say. And if you've found a group of friends that meshes perfectly with you, then maybe there isn't that much pressure to fit in, because you all fit together naturally.

But if you're like most teens, there's something about you that's a little different. Your friends like football, but you like hockey. Your friends like rock music but you like classical. Your friends are shy, but you're outgoing. Your friends are dog people, but you're a cat person. Or in a worst-case scenario, your friends are Team Edward, but you're Team Jacob.

Be brave. Be contradistinctive. Be different.

Don't hide from the world the aspects of you that are different, and certainly don't hide from your friends and family the aspects of you that are different. Embrace the things that make you original, and celebrate them as something that sets you apart from everyone else. Even if your friends laugh at you for your differences, laugh along with them! It's funny to be different.

There are several really nice benefits of being open about your differences:

- Being openly different exudes confidence, and builds even more confidence. And confidence is an extremely positive, attractive trait to have.

- Being openly different makes life more interesting for you, and for those around you. A conversation isn't very interesting or exciting if everyone agrees about the subject matter. But it gets a whole lot more interesting when there's a different viewpoint from somebody who just doesn't think like everyone else.

- Most importantly, being openly different makes you happier. It's really hard to keep a part of you that's different secret and hidden from the world. It's tough to be calm and stoic when you really want to laugh. It's difficult to sit in a chair and talk when you really feel like dancing. Some of the people in our society who probably feel the most pressure not to be different are members of the LGBTQ+ community. It's extra hard to pretend to like girls when you really like boys or vice versa. And those people in the LGBTQ+ community that have come out of the closet know firsthand how much happier it makes them to be openly different, and how emotionally difficult it is to keep their differences hidden.

Be contradistinctive. Be different. Embrace your differences. Wear your differences with pride and confidence. Let your differences make life more interesting. Let your differences shine so you can be happier.

#becontradistinctive

#bedifferent

#unique

#proudtobedifferent

"Why fit in when you were born to stand out?"

–Dr. Seuss

REMEMBER THAT YOU ONLY SEE EDITED LIVES

Everything you see on social media, television, and in the movies is edited to look as good as possible, so don't get fooled into being jealous or envious.

These days we have unprecedented access and insight into other people's lives. Fictional movies and TV shows bring us into the imagined world of doctors, lawyers, secret agents, and just plain normal people. Reality TV showcases the lives of real people from all over the world—and lets us see exactly what it's like to keep up with the Kardashians (Spoiler alert: it's absolutely awful). Most impactfully, social media brings us insight into the day-to-day lives of our friends and acquaintances.

With all this access and insight, it's easy to start comparing your own life to everybody else's. But it's important to remember that every photo you see on Instagram, every moment you watch on television, every video you catch on TikTok, and every post you read on Twitter, has been edited in some way, shape, or form. Images are staged and Photoshopped, videos are cut and reassembled, stories are planned out in advance—all to make sure that the unappealing, boring stuff gets eliminated, leaving only the crème de la crème.

For example, I saw a photo posted to Instagram of my good friend Archimedes Clutterbuck having a blast with a dozen of his friends at a huge, crazy party. I commented on the photo, "Looks like fun!" and thirty seconds later, my phone rang. It was Archimedes, calling from his car. "It was the most boring party I've ever had the displeasure to be stranded at," he said. "The most exciting guest at the party was the goldfish in the aquarium."

The actual party was in a small living room with twelve people sitting around in chairs, barely talking to each other. Archimedes was just about to leave out of sheer boredom when the host asked him and the others to get together for a photo. So Archimedes put his arms around the total strangers next to him, and smiled big. Immediately after the camera disappeared, Archimedes, still bored, left the party and went home.

But if you were on Instagram minutes later, all you saw was the 1/125 of a second that everybody looked like they were great friends, having an incredible time together at a crazy party. You didn't see the minutes, hours, and days of those people's lives where things were just humdrum and calm. And even more importantly, you didn't get to see the thoughts floating around the heads of all those people: the boredom, the insecurity, the loneliness, and the fear.

I'm sure you do the same thing. If somebody takes a photo of you when you're bored, you don't just sit there and stare blankly at the camera. You smile for a moment, let them snap the photo, and then go back to your boredom. Ninety-nine percent of the time, life probably isn't exciting enough to warrant a huge, crazy, grin on your face. But you want every photo and every video to look like the 1 percent of life that actually *is* pretty darn exciting, so you create an edited version of your life. That's what everybody does, and so that's what the world sees in people's social media feeds, in movies, and in TV shows: the 1 percent of life that is most exciting. Social media is the "Greatest Hits" album of our lives.

But there's one big exception. There's one life that you do get a full, unedited, inside view of: your own life.

Your life is the only unedited life you get to watch all day, every day, 100 percent of the time. Your life is the only one where you can hear every thought floating around inside your head. And most of your unedited life is the 99 percent of stuff that is boring and uneventful and not worthy of posting on Instagram, not the 1 percent of stuff that is exciting. Many of your thoughts probably aren't always positive, inspiring, and confident. In comparison to the 1 percent of edited lives you're seeing in other people's social media and on television, the bulk of your life probably seems to pale in comparison.

Even more importantly, you're missing 100 percent of what's going on INSIDE everybody's heads, which is a lot of insecurity, lack of confidence, and other problems. Very few people are vulnerable enough to share and show their problems to the world, so you'll NEVER have any idea of what is really going on in somebody's life, especially not from their social media.

There are a few takeaways from all of this. First, don't waste too much, or any, of your time watching other people's lives on social media or television. Why spend time watching other people's great memories, when you could be spending time creating your own?

Second, when you do see snippets of other people's lives, please don't compare your own unedited life to their edited "highlight reel." Their edited life is not real. It doesn't give the full story. You don't see all the unpublished moments, and all the thoughts inside their heads. And comparing your unedited life to their edited one isn't a fair comparison, and only serves to inspire jealousy and envy (two of the ugliest, most destructive emotions).

Stay away from watching other people's lives, and focus on your own. You'll be much happier for it.

#editedlife

#uneditedlife

#highlightreel

"Everyone you meet is fighting a battle you know nothing about."

–Ian Maclaren

BE A CREATOR, NOT A CONSUMER

Spend your free time creating new things for the world, rather than blindly consuming television shows, social media, sports, news, art, or movies.

Watching television is relaxing. Viewing social media is fun. The same goes for watching sports, news, movies, and lots of other things. And relaxation and fun are, well, relaxing and fun.

But realize that, with all these things, you're a watcher, a viewer, a consumer.

You're not a doer. You're not a creator.

Most of our actions in life boil down to one of these two categories: consuming or creating. At school, while listening to a teacher lecture, you're consuming. Later on, while doing your homework, you're creating. After that, while watching television or YouTube videos or looking at your friends' social media posts, you're consuming again.

Why is it so important to spend time creating, rather than just consuming? By creating, you're impacting people's lives and touching them. You're giving your life significance. You're changing the world, even if it's in an ever so tiny way.

Being a creator versus a consumer is similar to being a leader versus a follower. It's being a doer versus a watcher. It's a person who is fully involved in life and leaving their mark on the world by sharing their gifts and creating a better place for us all, versus a person who is satisfied taking what the world has to offer, not giving anything back, and being content just meandering through the world without ever having truly lived.

You don't have to be an artist or an inventor to create something of value to others. Anybody can create things. And almost everyone in the working world who earns a paycheck does create something. Your parents probably spend most of their time at work creating something of value, be it a product or a service. (Otherwise, it's likely that nobody would pay them to work!)

If you like photography, create by taking some photos. If you like writing, create by posting a blog entry. If you like programming, create by making a computer do something cool. If you like singing, create by writing, or just singing, a song. If you like astronomy, create by searching for a new comet. If you like science, create by conducting some experiments. Heck, if you like accounting, create by doing somebody's taxes.

Be open-minded about what "qualifies" as creating something. It's not just limited to making something you can hold in your hands, or see, or listen to. Just by talking to a friend, you're creating a closer relationship. By volunteering your time, you're creating happiness and a better world. By meditating, you're creating a more relaxed, focused mind-set. "Creating" can be almost anything that engages your mind and abilities, and doesn't involve you solely watching or listening to somebody else's creation.

This doesn't mean there isn't time to be a consumer. Of course there is. Heck, you're consuming this piece of Great Advice right now! And there are other amazing books, TV shows, movies, art, museums, and places around the world that demand to be consumed and will make you a better and happier person for having consumed them. And let's not forget memes. Gotta consume those memes, right?

Just make sure you balance your consumption with creation. And it's easy to create. You just have to turn off the television, get up off the couch, and share your gifts in some way.

If you want to give back to this world that you live in, consume less and create more.

#createdontconsume

#createmore

#shareyourgifts

"Creativity is the way I share my soul with the world."

–Brené Brown

THE IMAGES YOU POST DEFINE YOUR IMAGE FOREVER

Be careful what you post online because the revealing photos you post today will be on the internet forever. And years from now, you may not want them to be.

If you're on Instagram you've probably seen photos that were somewhat risqué or sexual in nature. Actually, if you're on Instagram, you've DEFINITELY seen photos that were somewhat risqué or sexual in nature.

Some of those photos are artistic in nature, and some of them are... less artistic. And when it comes right down to it, there's absolutely nothing wrong with celebrating the human body. Even if you've got a body shaped like mine.

Despite this fact, if you're thinking of taking some risqué photos of yourself, especially as a teenager, you might want to think long and hard before doing so.

Unless you've been living in a cave or without internet access for the past decade, you probably already know that what gets published on the internet stays on the internet. Forever. So when you take a photo that reveals your body to the world in a sexual way, the entire world gets to look at your body in a sexual way. Forever.

And so, before you do that, you have to ask yourself a few things:

1. Do I want the world to be able to see my body in a sexual way from now until the end of time?

2. What message about me do these photos send to people all over the world looking at them?

3. Am I sure I want to send that message to people all over the world forever and ever?

You probably already know exactly what sort of message a sexy photo of you sends to the world: I am attractive, I have a beautiful face, and I have a sexy body. And you probably already realize that the more people that see the photo and see how attractive you are, the more attention and admiration you will get. That all sounds great.

But is that really the type of attention and admiration you want? Is that really the type of attention and admiration you will want ten or twenty years from now?

If you publish photos of you posing in a sexy, revealing manner to show how attractive you are, don't be surprised if people looking at those photos think of you ONLY as somebody who is attractive. Don't be surprised if people looking at those photos think of you ONLY as a sexual object.

Because that's kind of the message you send when you take a photo that only focuses on your beauty and sexuality. You're unconsciously shouting from the rooftops, "My looks are the most important thing about me, not my personality, my athleticism, my intelligence, my humor, my business acumen, or anything else." Now if you think your beauty really *is* your most important quality, and that it will remain your most important quality for the rest of your life, then by all means, go ahead and take sexy photos that focus on your looks. But really? Do you really think that your looks are, and will always be, your most important quality?

Even the most beautiful, successful supermodels in the world usually build their brands around something other than their beauty. Kathy Ireland built a company around her taste in home décor and fashion. Heidi Klum launched successful fragrance and clothing lines, became a television producer, and is an accomplished painter. Chrissy Teigen is a best-selling author of cookbooks, and launched her own cookware line.

Before you post, think ahead. Think ahead ten years, and ask yourself if it's likely that the way you want your image to be perceived might change. (Hint: It's more than likely; it's almost a certainty.) Because in ten years from now, even if you decide that you want to be known for your business acumen instead of your beauty, there's a good chance that any sexy photos of you are always going to come up first in search results, rather than photos of the amazing building you designed, or photos of the groundbreaking product you invented, or photos of you on the cover of *Fortune* magazine celebrating your success.

If you do decide that you might one day want to be known for something other than your beauty and sexuality (can you tell yet that I think this is a good choice?), consider taking photos that are focused on things other than your beauty and sexuality. Take photos that focus on different aspects of your personality that portray a different image of yourself.

For instance, if you're at the beach, instead of taking photos of yourself in a fashionable swimsuit lying in a sexy pose on the sand, illustrating how beautiful you are, take a photo of yourself in a fashionable swimsuit surfing the waves, illustrating how adventurous you are. Or take a photo of yourself in a fashionable swimsuit reading at the beach, showing how intellectual you are. Or take a photo of yourself in a fashionable swimsuit swimming in the ocean, showing how athletic you are.

And while we're at it, it should be clear that this Great Advice applies not just to photos you post to your social media, but any photo you take. Because any photo you take, whether you share it with a friend or not (but especially if you share it with a friend), can end up being made public on the Internet forever.

You should consider every post to your online persona as helping to permanently define your own personal brand image. The key word is "permanently." Every selfie you post, every word you write, every opinion you publish, and every comment you make reveals to the entire world something about you, your values, your personality, and your opinions, and it remains public for the rest of time.

If a photo you're about to post doesn't portray you in the way you want to be portrayed, not just today but for the rest of your life, think twice before posting it.

#theinternetisforever

#mypersonalbrand

"If it's on the internet for one second, it's on the internet forever."

–Parry Aftab

STEP INTO THE ARENA

*Get out of your comfort zone
and take risks in life.*

Teens get embarrassed. A lot. I mean A LOT. I'm guessing you're embarrassed just reading this and knowing that I'm addressing you directly, right?

You probably care a lot about what your friends and acquaintances and family think about you. You probably even care about what crazy Aunt Edna thinks about you. And naturally, because you don't enjoy being embarrassed, you tend to try to minimize the amount of embarrassment you experience. That's to be expected. But it's such a shame.

It's a shame because one of the main side effects of trying to minimize the amount of embarrassment you experience is playing it safe. And playing it safe is an awful way to live your life—especially when you're a teen and the stakes of not playing it safe are so low.

Yes, yes, I fully appreciate the enormous risk you're taking by leaving the house with your hair looking like that (great mohawk, by the way). I understand that your life will be over if people ever hear what a terrible karaoke singer you are. I know that you will be ostracized from your community if anyone learns that you've been to seven Justin Bieber concerts (and perhaps you *should* be ostracized).

We all understand that the stakes are pretty high for a teen, and the risks you are sometimes tempted to take are big ones. But I have to let you in on a secret: When you compare these risks to some of the risks you'll be taking when you're an adult, they pale in comparison. And so…

Learn to take risks. Learn to take lots of risks. Now. While you don't have much to lose. And let me assure you that, if you don't have a spouse or kids to take care of, and if you do have parents that are around to support you emotionally and financially, then you really do not have much to lose.

Try out for the cross-country team! I know, if you do, you risk the embarrassment of being the slowest person on the team, and having to hang your head in shame each time you come in last place, and endure the taunts of everyone on the team calling you "The Tortoise." But if you don't try out for the team, play it safe, and sit on the sidelines, you risk the silent torture of watching everyone else enjoy the thrill of competition week after week, and wondering if you could have beaten them all if only you had just taken a risk.

Raise your hand in class when the teacher asks a tough question! I know, if you do, you risk a few moments of shame when you answer "The Battle of Gettysburg" when the question your math teacher asked was, "What is the square root of forty-nine?" But if you remain silent and don't raise your hand, you risk letting another student answer the question, giving the exact same answer that you would've given, and hearing the accolades of the teacher saying to somebody else, "So impressive that you knew that answer!"

Take it from President Teddy Roosevelt, the eight-time winner of the prestigious "best presidential mustache" award, who said (paraphrasing), "The people who criticize others do not count. The credit belongs to the person who steps into the arena, whose face is marred by dust and sweat and blood, who tries valiantly, and who, at best, knows the triumph of winning, and at worst, fails while daring greatly. That person never has to worry about being one of those frightened critics who doesn't ever win or lose because they never even tried."

As good ol' Teddy says, step into the arena! As long as the risks you take are not dangerous or irreparable, take those risks! Don't sit on the sidelines when you could be in the arena playing the game. Being in the arena is exhilarating. Being in the arena is exciting. Being in the arena is fun. Being in the arena means you have the chance to experience all of that, and win big. Being in the arena means that, even if you lose, you had an amazing experience, became stronger in the process, and did more than every other person sitting on the sidelines, watching you compete in the arena.

Step into the arena. Take some risks.

#takerisks

#stepintothearena

#riskit

#failwhiledaringgreatly

"Take risks. If you win, you will be happy. If you lose, you will be wise."

–Unknown

DON'T NEGLECT YOUR FRIENDS FOR YOUR SIGNIFICANT OTHER

It's great to spend lots of time with your boyfriend/ girlfriend, but make it a point to always spend some time with your friends.

In high school, my good friend Archimedes Clutterbuck didn't have the most active dating life. That's a nice way of saying that he didn't have a dating life at all. But then, on one of those rare days that he happened to dress respectably, comb his hair, AND brush his teeth, he happened to meet a girl who was looking for a guy just like him. And that was the last time my friends and I saw Archimedes for eight months.

He spent every available moment with that girl, and didn't spend any time with us. He was the happiest he had ever been in his life... until she broke up with him. He went from the highest high to the lowest low. And when you're at your lowest, that's when you need a friend the most.

But Archimedes had abandoned all his friends, and so not only did he no longer have a girlfriend, but he no longer had any friends. It was a lonely time for him. Luckily though, when he needed his friends the most, we all took him back, re-established our friend-ship, and helped him through the rough patch.

But sometimes other people aren't so lucky.

If you've got a boyfriend or girlfriend, congratulations! You're probably really happy to have a special person in your life to share things with, and your friends are probably really happy to see you so happy.

And because you like this special person so much, you probably enjoy spending a lot of time with them, and you probably enjoy spending time with them so much that you want to spend as much time with them as possible. It's great to like somebody so much that you can't ever get enough of them. It's a rare thing, and if you have that in your life, be grateful. But don't make the same mistake Archimedes made.

Don't neglect your friends.

If you're the type of person who wants to spend as much time with your significant other as possible, then you might also find that you don't have the time to see your friends as much. Or barely at all.

The most common fight between friends is, "You spend so much time with that person that you never spend time with me anymore."

On the one hand, when you start dating somebody, it's perfectly fair and normal to want to spend a lot of time with them. And since science has proven beyond the shadow of a doubt that there are still only twenty-four hours in a day, simple math says that if you increase the amount of time you spend with your significant other, you'll have to decrease the amount of time you used to spend on other things, including your friends.

On the other hand, it's important that you don't completely eliminate all your time with your friends. Because let's face it, friends that you don't spend time with aren't really friends. They're people you used to be friends with.

I must say that it's obvious to anybody looking at you and your significant other how in love you both are and how perfect you are for each other, and it's clear that your significant other is, for sure, 100 percent, absolutely, positively your soulmate who you will spend the rest of your life with and probably the next life too. However...

The numbers seem to prove out that most teens (not you, of course, but most) end up dating many different people over the course of their dating lives. Boyfriends and girlfriends come and go, but friends, especially best friends, stick around for a lifetime (hopefully). However, it doesn't take a rocket scientist to realize if you neglect your friends when you're dating somebody, then when you stop dating that person, you might find that not only did you lose the person you were dating, but you also lost your friends. And some friends, once they're gone, don't come back.

So, even though you'd rather spend every minute of every day with your significant other, make the effort to still spend a good amount of time with your friends. And make sure that when you *do* spend time with your friends, you're 100 percent focused on them (and not texting your significant other, or constantly talking about them).

And while we're at it, this Great Advice applies to all other aspects of your life too. When you start dating somebody, don't let your grades slip. Don't give up your hobbies and interests. Don't ignore your parents. And don't give up having some "alone time" with just yourself.

It's great to enjoy time with your significant other. Just always leave some time for other important things in your life, especially your friends.

#friendsfirst

#friendsforever

*"The only way
to have a friend
is to be one."*

–Ralph Waldo Emerson

GREAT ADVICE #11

LEARN HOW TO APOLOGIZE

> *When you make a mistake, swallow your pride and apologize. You'll be amazed at what a difference it makes.*

I'm sorry.

There, I said it. I'm sorry if this book isn't as good as you had hoped. I'm sorry if the Great Advice I'm giving isn't quite as great as it should be. Or worse, I'm sorry if it's actually bad advice and caused you some pain. I'm sorry, and I'll do my best to make the next piece of advice truly Great. Speaking of my next piece of Great Advice, here it is....

Learn how to apologize.

One of the hardest skills that teenagers, and most adults, need to learn is how to apologize. We live in a culture in which showing weakness is generally not rewarded. We live in a culture in which lawyers will advise you that, if you apologize, you're admitting guilt and will lose your court case. We live in a culture in which everyone from the President of the United States down to a customer service representative on the phone never wants to admit they screwed up. And the strange thing is that we all know that *everyone* screws up every once in a while.

It certainly isn't easy to admit you were wrong, but I'll tell you this... it makes a lot of wrong situations right very quickly. Most people don't ever expect anybody else to admit they were wrong and apologize, so when you actually do apologize, something amazing usually happens. Apologizing throws people off balance. Apologizing surprises people. And nine times out of ten, apologizing causes people to have a hard time staying angry at you. Why? When you do something wrong to somebody, you can't usually take it back. You usually only have two options:

1. Try to convince the other person that what you did wasn't really that bad, or it wasn't really your fault, or some other reason why they shouldn't be angry with you. This strategy isn't usually successful, since the other person is already angry, and all you're really doing is trying to convince them not to be angry.

2. Simply apologize for what you did. This strategy usually IS successful because, once you apologize to somebody and admit you did something wrong, and convince them you wish you hadn't done it and will do your best not to do it again, there's nothing more you really can do or say. The ball is now in their court, and the only remaining option open to them is to remain angry at you forever, or eventually forgive you. As long as what you did isn't an "unforgivable" sin, most people you come across will choose the forgiveness route, rather than the stay-angry-at-you-forever route.

It used to be that when doctors made serious medical errors, their lawyers would not allow them to apologize, because it would be admitting fault and cause them to lose any case brought to court. Patients who were paralyzed during routine surgeries, or family members of patients accidentally killed during routine procedures, would never be told that a doctor's mistake caused the problem. They would never be given details of what happened, and would never be issued an apology for the mistake. Patients would sue the "cold-hearted" hospital, in large part because nobody from the hospital ever said those two simple words: "I'm sorry."

Recently though, many hospitals changed their policies, and now, when a doctor makes a medical error, they admit the error, describe how it happened, and most importantly, apologize for the mistake. The response by patients has been so much more favorable because of the apology that they end up accepting reasonable settlements from the hospital without any lawsuits, and in some cases, refuse to take money from the hospital at all. These apologies are so effective at making both doctor and patient feel better that there are now "apology laws" in thirty-nine states that enable doctors to apologize without that apology being used against them if there is a lawsuit later filed.

My good friend Archimedes Clutterbuck got into a car accident in which he rear-ended another driver. The crash was totally and completely his fault. The other driver quickly got out of his car and ran over screaming his head off, telling Archie what an idiot he was. Now many people might have screamed right back, blaming the other driver for braking too quickly, or trying to come up with some other reason why it was the other person's fault.

But Archimedes took a different approach. He said, "I'm so sorry, are you okay?" The other driver continued on, spouting, "What kind of a moron are you?" Archie repeated, "I'm so sorry, are you okay?" In an instant, the driver relented, calmed down, and said, "Yeah, I'm okay." And then, in an amazing turn of events, the driver asked Archimedes, "Are *you* okay?"

A guy whose car was violently smashed, who was furiously screaming his head off moments earlier, who was expecting the other driver to try to avoid blame, immediately calmed down and became empathetic, just because of a simple apology from another human being.

Apologies can go a long way in righting lots of wrongs. But it's important to make sure that, when apologizing for something, you do it right:

- Make your apologies sincere. If it looks like the apology was forced, or made simply for pragmatic reasons, it's useless. And even a slight hint of rolling your eyes while you apologize is worse than no apology at all.

- Please, please, please don't dilute your apology with an excuse, or by secretly blaming the other person with something like, "I'm sorry you're angry with me for doing what I did." That type of apology belongs in the Hall of Fame of terrible apologies. If your apology includes the word "but," it's not an apology.

- Don't just give a simple, "I'm sorry." It's better to say, "I'm sorry for doing 'X' and I'll try to do 'Y' in the future so it doesn't happen again." That shows that you understand what you did was wrong, why it was wrong, and more importantly, you have a plan to ensure it doesn't happen again. (Oh, and you should actually, sincerely try to make sure it doesn't happen again.)

Swallow your pride and be human. We all make mistakes. When you do make a mistake, simply apologize. You'll be amazed at what a difference it makes.

And if you disagree with me, I'm sorry.

#saysorry

#greatapologies

#imsorry

"An apology is the super glue of life. It can repair just about anything."

–Lynn Johnston

DON'T FEAR YOUR CRUSH, CRUSH YOUR FEAR

Stop wondering if they like you. Get past your fear of embarrassment and make a move on your crush. It's worth the risk.

There are lots of things that aren't great about being a teenager. You're smarter than your parents, but you still have to listen to them. You don't get any privacy. And don't get me started on your teachers.

But one of the greatest things about being a teenager is arriving at the stage of life where you start liking people. "But I've always liked people," you say. I'm not talking about liking people; I'm talking about "liking" people! Boyfriends, girlfriends, crushes. (Wink, wink.)

The thing that contributes most to your happiness in life probably isn't what you think it is. It's not money. It's not your grades or future career. It's not even being famous. It's your relationships. Not only your relationships with your friends and family, but also your relationship with that one person in your life who you're closest with: a boyfriend, girlfriend, significant other, partner, better half, ball and chain, bae, crush, companion, sweetheart, boo, paramour, soulmate, true love, or anything else you want to call them.

Is it necessary to have a significant other to be happy? Nope. Friends and family do the trick for lots and lots of people. In fact, it's estimated that about 1 percent of the population don't have any interest at all in romantic or sexual relationships.

But for the rest of us that do, our crushes can be the most exciting part of our lives. I believe (as do many others) that finding that special somebody who lights your fire is the most rewarding, important, exciting, valuable, and special aspect of most people's lives. More than your career. More than money. More than almost anything else I can think of, except perhaps having kids (which, as you may know, is a byproduct of having that special somebody).

So if you're at the stage where you "like" someone and have a crush, especially if it's your first crush, you're probably amazingly exhilarated and amazingly terrified at the same time. Exhilarated at the prospect that your crush might like you too, but terrified at the prospect that your crush might not feel the same. Or maybe even more terrified at the prospect that your crush WILL like you.

If you're like a lot of teens, this feeling of being terrified usually wins out over the feeling of exhilaration, and as a result, you might go out of your way to make sure that your crush never finds out about your feelings. After all, if that person discovers your feelings, you risk the chance that maybe they just want to be friends, and OMG, you'll experience a level of embarrassment and sadness and disappointment never seen before by anyone on this planet. (Except by the other few billion people who have also been rejected by somebody they like.)

It's true. Having a crush on somebody who doesn't feel the same kind of sucks. And it sucks so bad that I can't blame you for not wanting to let your crush know that you like them. But the problem is that, as much as it sucks to find out your crush doesn't like you the way you like them, there's something that sucks ten times more than that....

Not doing anything while your crush secretly has the exact same feelings about you as you have about them. That really sucks. That worse than sucks. That supersucks.

It supersucks when another day goes by that you could be spending together with your crush, at a level of happiness you've probably never experienced before, but instead you both remain apart, cowering in fear. It supersucks wondering each and every day, for weeks, and months, and maybe even years, whether or not your crush likes you, hoping they'll take the risk that you're too afraid to take and say something first, revealing their true feelings for you. It supersucks finding out at your high school reunion twenty years later that you both had a major crush on each other, but neither one of you did anything about it, and missed out on something really special.

Having a special, romantic relationship with somebody is the stuff life is made of. I'd even go so far as to say that it's kind of the whole reason we've been put here on this planet. It's so amazing that you can't sit around in fear doing nothing, while the chance of experiencing a relationship like that passes you by. You must do something. You have to make things happen. You have to find out.

Tell your crush you like them.

Or if that's too scary for you, do something bold to build a relationship with them. Sit down next to them at lunchtime. Text them a joke. Share a doughnut. Watch a video together. Ask if they want to do homework with you. Invite them to a movie. Ask them to dance.

If they don't feel the same about you, you'll experience a little bit of disappointment and sadness (and maybe even some embarrassment), but you'll also have the benefit of not wasting any more time on a relationship that won't happen, and be able to move on to building a relationship with somebody new that *is* interested.

But...

If they do feel the same about you, you'll experience one of the absolute best things you can possibly experience in this life of yours. Crush your fear. Tell your crush you like them. Now.

#crushyourfear

#tellyourcrush

#supersucks

#tellhim

#tellher

"If you don't go after what you want, you'll never have it."

–Nora Roberts

INTERMISSION

YOU DESERVE A BREAK... AND A REWARD

You're halfway through the book. I hope you've enjoyed all the Great Advice so far. Fortunately, there's more to come! But it takes a lot of focus and energy to take in all this Great Advice at once, so before we get back to it, take a well-deserved, short break. Take a deep breath. Stretch your legs. Get a snack. Look at some memes. You deserve a meme!

Not only do you deserve a break, but you deserve a reward too. But what reward could I possibly give you that would be better than the Great Advice I've already given you and the Great Advice to come? How can I raise my game to give you something that truly rewards you and expresses the sincere gratitude I have that you're even holding, let alone reading, this book?

I wracked my brain, pulled out all the stops, and finally figured out something even better than Great Advice....

[Insert sound of trumpets blaring here]

The Top 10 Greatest Great Advice of All Time!

That's right. Not good advice. Not Great Advice. But the *Top 10 Greatest Great Advice of All Time*, as recently voted on by our readers (and me). I'll send it to you right now if you just email me at:

marc@greatadvicegroup.com

or if you prefer, visit

greatadvicegroup.com/top10advice2

And by the way, along with the *Top Ten Greatest Great Advice of All Time*, don't be surprised if I also send you some of my favorite memes as well, OK?

Speaking of memes...

Do you need more memes? We got 'em! Got some better memes? We want 'em!

Check out our Great Advice Meme Hall of Fame, or submit your own at:

greatadvicegroup.com/memes2

YOU WILL BECOME YOUR FRIENDS

Choose your friends wisely because the people you spend the most time with are likely to be the type of person you will soon become.

You might wish you were somebody other than who you are—someone better-looking, less fat, more muscular, more fashionable, more popular, smarter, faster, cooler, nicer, or something else. You might look at other teens you know, and wish you could be more "like them." You might think that, if you could be friends with them, you actually would be more "like them."

Be careful what you wish for.

It's great to want to be a better person, and to want to improve yourself. And it's great to aspire to be friends with people who can help you become that person.

For instance, maybe you're like a lot of teens and you want be more "popular." After all, being popular looks great from the outside. It's like the popular kids have been granted celebrity status. Sometimes it's because they're more athletic than others; sometimes because they're better-looking than others; and sometimes for no good reason at all (I'm talking to you, Kim Kardashian). And maybe you become friends with the popular people, which helps you become more popular too. Everything's great!

75

But it's possible that, in your yearning to be friends with the popular kids, you focused so much on their popularity that it overshadowed other qualities about your friends that maybe you don't like so much. Your new friends might be really popular, but do they treat other people poorly? Do they drink, smoke, vape, or do drugs? Do they show disrespect to their teachers and parents? And if so, are those really the qualities you want in a friend?

Hang out with the right crowd.

Don't be so blinded by somebody's popularity, beauty, athleticism, or fashion sense, that you get comfortable overlooking some of their negative qualities. Because if you befriend somebody with negative qualities, the chances are very good that you will eventually adopt those negative qualities yourself. You might not think that's possible, but I promise you, it's true.

When my good friend Archimedes Clutterbuck was in high school, he helped tutor a group of students who were having trouble in math, primarily because, instead of studying math, they went to parties and drank beer. He slowly built a friendship with this group of guys, and eventually started going to parties with his new friends, although he never drank at those parties. His friends didn't put any pressure on him to drink (primarily because they liked having their own designated driver), and yet, after going to enough parties where Archimedes was surrounded by people drinking beer, he decided to drink too. And after a few more of these parties, he, like his new friends, got busted for underage drinking and spent a night in jail.

He didn't realize it at the time, because his behavior changes were so gradual, but he had become exactly the type of person that his friends were. And it wasn't the type of person he wanted to be. Luckily, he was smart enough to realize how he was changing, and smart enough to break it off with that group of friends before he got into any more trouble. But the key takeaway from his experience is if your friends smoke and drink, you will probably soon smoke and drink. If your friends do dangerous drugs, you will probably soon do dangerous drugs. If your friends tease other people, you will probably start to tease other people. If your friends talk back to their teachers and parents, you will probably begin to talk back to your teachers and parents. If your friends constantly get into trouble, you will probably start to get into trouble.

"But I'm not going to do any of that, even if my friends do," you protest.

Well, guess what. Even if you don't do any of those things, just by hanging out with people who do, you can get into as much trouble as they do. If you're at a party where people are doing illegal drugs, when the police show up, even if you didn't do illegal drugs, you're going to end up in the back of the police cruiser anyway.

"Good point," you say. "So I just won't stick around when that kind of stuff happens."

Guess again. Even if you're not around when your friends do that sort of stuff, by hanging out with them, their reputation becomes yours. If you hang out with the kids who drink, smoke, and vape, everyone will assume that you drink, smoke, and vape as well. If you hang out with the kids who bully other kids, everyone will assume that you bully other kids.

Sometimes, it might not be so obvious to you that you're hanging out with the wrong crowd. Maybe your friends aren't drinking, or smoking, or vaping, or doing drugs, but they're doing other subtler things that aren't compatible with your own personality and values. Pay attention to the warning signs:

- Have you ever been embarrassed by something your friends did?
- Have you been ashamed of something they did?
- Have you ever gotten in trouble because of something they did?
- Did you ever do something stupid because of their influence?

- Are you keeping your friendships secret from others because you're embarrassed or ashamed?

If you answered yes to any of these questions, think long and hard about whether you're hanging out with the right crowd.

The more time you spend with your friends, the more similar to those friends you will become. So choose your friends wisely, and make sure that the people you spend the most time with are the type of person that you are, or want to become.

#chooseyourfriendswisely

#youareyourfriends

#findthegoodones

"You can't soar like an eagle when you hang out with turkeys."

–Unknown

TRY EVERYTHING

Live life to the fullest and try everything at least once. It will change you as a person.

When you were a baby, you had a lot of "first time" experiences: The first time you rolled over, the first time you ate mashed peas, the first time you pooped mashed peas. There's a reason that some of the most viral videos are those of a baby's look of excitement while sucking on a lemon for the first time, or standing up for the first time. One of the most exciting things about being a baby, a toddler, a pre-teen, or a teenager, is the excitement of doing things for the first time, and those babies remind us how excited we used to get from experiences that now seem boring and mundane.

You're probably not that excited about sucking on a lemon or standing up anymore. (At least I hope you're not.) But there are still a lot of firsts out there for teens. There's the first time you drive, the first time you vote, the first time you kiss somebody, the first time you climb a mountain, the first time you waterski, the first time you skydive. The list is endless.

"But... it's scary," you say.

Yes! That's the whole point. It's scary to drive for the first time. It's scary to climb a mountain for the first time. It's scary to skydive for the first time. It is scary. And it may seem dangerous. But remember this: Almost anything you do that sounds scary and seems dangerous isn't really that dangerous if you go about doing it in a smart way. And a smart way usually means doing it for the first time with the assistance and guidance of somebody more experienced than you.

For instance, if you want to skydive, and you decide to just strap on a parachute and jump out of an airplane, perhaps you really should be scared. On the other hand, if you hire an experienced instructor to take you on a tandem skydive, with you strapped firmly to their chest, and then you go through hours and hours of training and testing before actually jumping out of an airplane on your own, your level of danger is reduced significantly.

Fear, however, is not the only thing you'll feel when you do something for the first time. You'll also feel an unparalleled excitement that quickly overpowers the fear—a flow of adrenaline coursing through your body that you don't get with many other things. And this excitement alone is reason enough to try new things that you've never done before. It contributes toward living an exciting and passionate life.

But there are lots of other reasons to try new things. For one, you're young. Too young to be set in your ways. Too young to be closing your mind to new experiences. Too young to be saying "I'm not a skydiver," or "I don't like climbing mountains." Be open to trying new things, and you'll probably find that you will experience things that change your routine, change your opinion of things, change the way you look at the world, and in general, change you in unpredictable ways.

And if nothing else, if you try something new and don't like it… well, that's one thing that you now know you don't like, and one thing that you now don't have to wonder about liking anymore.

I hope it goes without saying, but just to be clear, when I say "Try new things," I don't mean you should try absolutely everything. There are a bunch of dangerous, illegal, or immoral things that don't ever need to be tried: heroin, robbing a bank, cheating on your boyfriend/girlfriend, punching somebody. You should obviously take a pass on these things.

But if it's unlikely to hurt you, or anybody else, then do yourself a favor and try it. Just once.

Broaden your horizons! Suck the marrow out of life! Try new things! There's a really good chance you'll be happy you did.

#tryeverything

#tryit

#suckthemarrow

"Twenty years from now, you will be more disappointed by the things you didn't do than by the things you did do."

–Unknown

DON'T TRUST YOUR BRAIN TO MAKE DECISIONS

Trust your gut. Even though we don't yet know how or why, sometimes your intuition is smarter than your brain.

If you look back at all the crazy things people thought were true just a few hundred years ago, those people look like idiots. They used to think drinking mercury was good for you. (It's not. It will kill you.) They used to think bloodletting using leeches was a good idea to get rid of infections. (It isn't. It's disgusting.) They used to think the world is flat. (It isn't. But some people still aren't convinced.)

Of course, this means that we're all going to look like idiots to the people of the future. "Those dolts didn't even know how to levitate!" they'll say.

One of the crazier things scientists recently discovered may be true is that the idea of "trusting your gut" to help you make decisions actually works. They've discovered that our human bodies and other living creatures are capable of sensing things we don't even realize we're sensing. The human body really does have something called "intuition" or a "gut feeling," and it ends up being right significantly more than 50 percent of the time. Our bodies are capable of knowing some things that we don't consciously know ourselves.

Unfortunately, these scientists don't yet know *how* this happens, but thankfully, we don't really need to know how it happens to use this little superpower of ours. And so my Great Advice to you is...

Always trust your gut.

Understand and accept that, somehow, your brain and body are working on levels that you can't consciously understand, but can feel nevertheless. So learn to feel it. Learn to feel your gut. And more importantly, learn to trust your gut. It's usually right.

It can be frustrating to hear "trust your gut" if you don't think you can feel your "gut" or "intuition." Admittedly, it's hard to get in touch with your gut, especially as a teen. It's not something that happens overnight, but here's one tactic you can use that has worked for me.

Let's say you're faced with a decision of whether to join the school play or the tennis team (you can't do both). You're likely to do some sort of informal list of pros and cons for each option, and then use that list to help make your decision. If that works for you, great. But if you make your little list of pros and cons and still feel like things are evenly balanced, then you have to defer to your gut. Here's how to do it:

Flip a coin.

Heads means you do the school play, tails means you join the tennis team. Decide ahead of time that you're going to commit to whatever it is that fate decides for you. Then when you flip that coin and look at the result, take stock of the immediate feeling you get. If you get a reaction of relief and happiness, then follow the coin. But if you look at the coin and think, *Best out of three?* that's your gut speaking to you. Listen to your gut and tell that stupid coin to go jump in a lake.

Listening to your gut is easier said than done, I know. But it's also a skill you can get better at. Years ago, my good friend Archimedes Clutterbuck got into a very prestigious college, as well as a smaller college that he applied to just because the campus felt right. He turned down the prestigious college for the one that felt right to his gut, and never regretted his decision.

Later in life, Archie had to hire a graphic designer to create a logo. One candidate had years of experience, while another, though less experienced, seemed to click with Archie creatively. Against his gut, he chose the more experienced person, and ended up getting a terrible result and regretting it. He later hired the more inexperienced person and got a logo that he loved.

As you try to listen to your gut more, you'll get better at hearing it and following it. And when you do, you'll probably start to notice some amazing results. In fact, I recommend you try a little experiment.

Start keeping track of major decisions you make—particularly decisions where you really want to decide one thing, but because of logical evidence or other people's opinions, you are tempted to do another thing. Write down what your gut tells you to do, what your head tells you to do, and the decision you ultimately make.

Then once the decision plays itself out, be it days, weeks, or months later, ask yourself if things turned out well with that decision, or if you'd view the decision as a bad one.

I can tell you that, for the past few years, Archimedes has been tracking these times that his "gut" didn't necessarily agree with what his head was telling him. And I was amazed when he told me that, without exception, when he trusted his gut, things ended up moving in a positive direction. And without exception, when he ignored his gut and decided to trust his brain, things didn't go well. Pretty convincing stuff, huh?

So, trust your gut. Listen to your intuition. Because even though we don't yet understand why or how, it seems certain that your gut is often smarter than your brain.

#trustyourgut

#gutoverbrain

#intuitionwins

"Trust your instincts. Your intuition doesn't lie."

–Oprah Winfrey

START YOUR CAREER NOW

Figure out what it is you want to do in life, and then start doing fun things that move you toward that career now.

Many people spend about nine years in elementary and middle school, four years in high school, four years in college, and then, after they graduate college, they begin their career.

Why wait?

If one of the goals of school is to prepare you for a career you're going to enjoy, why treat it like an all-or-nothing proposition? Why wait until you graduate college to start working on that career of yours? Start figuring out what you want to do in life now, and start working toward that goal now. Find the thing that lights your fire, and throw yourself fully into whatever that is.

To be clear, I'm not advising you to quit school and begin working a real job. There's time enough for real work when you're older. I'm talking about doing fun work! I am advocating that you think about what you want to do for a career, and find something that you can do that is fun, and excites you, while also moving you toward trying out that career, getting some experience, and most of all, learning something new.

It's not hard to move down that path. You don't have to wait until you're an adult. Teens sometimes have inferiority complexes about their age, thinking that they have nothing to offer the world until they've become an adult, studied, practiced, and have some baseline level of experience in their career. Nothing could be further from the truth.

In fact, it's quite the opposite. Nobody has more energy and more free time to use that energy than teenagers. At no time in your life will you ever have the freedom, the drive, the excitement, the creativity, the curiosity, and most importantly, the ability to work for the experience rather than the money, that you do today. And all those qualities happen to be quite valuable in the real world.

For instance, my good friend Archimedes Clutterbuck's thirteen-year-old daughter was interested in becoming an interior designer, so she started designing imaginary rooms of her own just for fun. Then one day, Archimedes heard that one of his friends was redoing his living room. His daughter didn't ask permission, she just drew up a dozen living room designs and gave those designs to Archie's friend for free. He was very complimentary of the designs, thanked her profusely for the ideas, and she was really flattered. But then two weeks later, he called back to tell her that he actually used one of her designs. In my book, that officially makes her an interior designer—at the age of thirteen!

If you want to be an inventor, start inventing stuff. If you want to be a scientist, start doing your own experiments, or volunteer in a lab. If you want to be a doctor, volunteer at a hospital. If you want to be an artist, start creating art. If you want to be a programmer, start writing programs. If you want to be a game designer, start designing games. If you want to be a... well, you get the point.

There are websites like Fiverr and Upwork where people look for inexpensive services from people all around the world. If you love doing things like designing logos, writing blog posts, translating foreign languages, drawing illustrations, doing 3D design, writing music, programming computers, or making animations, there are thousands of people on those websites looking for people to help them do those things and more. Sign up and offer your services. Even though you have the disadvantage of not having a lot of experience in those areas, you have the huge advantage of being able to significantly underprice all the adults offering those services. (And nothing feels better than stealing a sale from an experienced adult!) The worst-case scenario is that your customer doesn't like the work you do, and you refund their money. The best-case scenario is that they love your work and keep hiring you over and over and you build out your portfolio while making a little money on the side for your college fund.

At some point you might realize you don't really enjoy doing what you thought it is you want to do. Great! You now know of one career that you don't want to do, and can pivot to some other career that might interest you.

Remember that nobody says you have to get your career choice right on the first try. Or the second try. Or the third, fourth, fifth, sixth or seventh try. But rather than putting off a decision to figure out what you want to do until after college, take your best guess and work toward that goal in a way that's fun and exciting to you now.

In the end, while grades are important, they're not all that's important. It's helpful to learn about calculus and history and how to be a good writer, but it's also advantageous to figure out what excites you, become passionate about that thing, and spend some of your free time having fun and getting better at it.

Don't make the mistake of waiting until you're much older to start. Start doing fun, exciting things related to your future career today.

#startyourcareernow

#teencareers

#hireteens

"If you want to achieve greatness, stop asking for permission."

–Unknown

REMEMBER THAT IT ALWAYS GETS BETTER

When things are bad, you've lost all hope, and only see despair, remember that eventually the pain always ends and life returns to normal.

Life is tough. Being a teenager is tough.

Certainly, you've had some bad days in your life and, if you're like most teenagers, you've had some bad weeks or months. Maybe you got really sick. Maybe you were bullied at school. Maybe your parents were mean to you, or you were overweight, or you got a bad grade, or your girlfriend or boyfriend broke up with you, or your best friend betrayed you, or you had an eating disorder, or a drinking problem, or a drug problem, or you were depressed. Or perhaps worse than any of that, maybe nobody "liked" your Instagram post, god forbid.

There's no shortage of problems to go around for teenagers these days. And when you're in the middle of one of those problems, it can sometimes feel like you're at the lowest of lows. It can feel incredibly painful. And when you're at one of the lowest of lows, the natural tendency is to think about how bad your current situation is, and how hard it's going to be to survive another minute, or day, or week, or month with this hanging over your head.

But if you've been through something traumatic before and made it through to the other side, then you've learned one of the most important life lessons there is to know: The pain eventually ends and life returns to some sense of normalcy.

Thousands of years ago, the Persians used the phrase, "This too shall pass." Today, one of the more common phrases is, "Time heals all wounds." Probably the best one is from the LGBTQ+ community, who have adopted the phrase, "It gets better." And it's absolutely true. It does get better. It always gets better. And that's never truer than when you're at the lowest of lows, because if you're at the lowest of lows, there's nowhere to go but up.

When you're down, whatever you're going through, the chances are good that lots and lots of other people have gone through a similar situation, survived, and recovered enough to put it behind them. You should remind yourself that, if they made it through that storm, you can make it through too. Remembering that is often the most important thing to help you weather that storm.

The only possible way this advice is not true, the only possible way it doesn't get better... is if you give up. The only possible way this advice isn't true is if you end your life.

Most people who are suicidal can't possibly see how it will get better. They can't possibly see how it will pass; they can't possibly see how time will heal the wound. But if you talk to anybody who was suicidal, but somehow found the strength not to act in their moment of despair, 100 percent of them will testify to the fact that things got better, the bad times passed, and the wounds healed.

Is it easy to see that in the moment? Sometimes, no. It's easy to think that your problem is so bad, and so painful, that the pain will last forever. But I can tell you for a fact that it won't.

It always gets better.

If you have trouble remembering that, talk to a friend, a teacher, a parent, an adult, or a stranger, and they will remind you and convince you that...

It always gets better.

Even if you feel all alone, and you think you don't have a friend, a teacher, a parent, an adult, or even a stranger who will listen or understand, call The Suicide Prevention Hotline, and they will remind and convince you that...

It always gets better.

When things are bad, when you're at your worst, when you've lost all hope and only see despair, remember that...

It always gets better.

Even if you think you're the exception, and that your particular problem is insurmountable and won't ever get better, I promise you, you're wrong, because...

It always gets better.

It. Always. Gets. Better.

If you're thinking about suicide, please call The Suicide Prevention Hotline immediately at 1-800-273-8255 or visit

suicidepreventionlifeline.org

#italwaysgetsbetter

#thistooshallpass

#weatherthestorm

"*Even the darkest clouds have the sun behind them.*"

–Ashley Ballard

PUT YOURSELF IN OTHERS' SHOES

Empathy is the most important character trait you can develop, and is a skill that will help you become less judgmental and more understanding of people.

One of the hardest character traits to develop as you get older is empathy. At its most basic level, empathy is a learnable skill that gives you the ability to understand what someone else is feeling. It's not necessarily what you would feel in the same situation, but what the other person is actually feeling.

Although people confuse the two a great deal, empathy is significantly different than sympathy. Researcher Brené Brown put it nicely when she said that empathy drives connection between two people, while sympathy drives disconnection between two people. In other words, empathy makes someone feel like you understand how they feel and even feel a bit of it yourself. You share their pain and feel a bit of their pain yourself. On the other hand, sympathy makes someone feel like you know what they're going through and feel sorry for them, the subtext being that you're secretly grateful that you're not going through the same thing. You understand their pain, but you don't feel the pain yourself. It's easy to feel sympathy for somebody. Empathy is a much more difficult skill to develop.

But it's an important skill to develop because empathy is at the core of that Golden Rule by which we all try to live our lives: *Do unto others as you would have them do unto you.* Or in more modern terms: Treat others how you would like to be treated.

At the heart of empathy is the idea that, if you can't understand the trials and tribulations and pain and suffering that someone else goes through, then you can't expect others to share in and help with your own problems when you encounter them. And without that empathy for each other, the world becomes a very lonely place for us all to live in—a place where everyone is just on their own, out for themselves. Not many people want to live in that world.

Empathy is a cure for a lot of the world's evils. And closer to home, empathy is a cure for one of teenagers' biggest issues: being judgmental. If you're like most people, you typically judge other people when they say or do things differently than you do. You judge other people by saying, "I would never do what they did, because I'm better than that." But when you have empathy for a person, when you can see things from their perspective, it becomes significantly harder to judge them, and easier for you to understand how and why they're doing what it is they're doing. It makes you think, *I wonder what I might do in a similar situation, and whether people would have empathy for me or stand in judgment.*

For example, when my good friend Archimedes Clutterbuck was a young kid in sixth grade, he witnessed a boy being bullied at school. Most of the other students who had never been bullied, and didn't know firsthand how it felt to be bullied, didn't have much empathy for the bullied boy, and instead, judged him a bit. They felt like he was weak-minded for not sticking up for himself and fighting back.

But Archimedes had been bullied himself, so it was easier for him to be empathetic, remembering back to the pain he once felt, and feeling that pain again firsthand (even though it wasn't him being bullied this time). Instead of judging the boy as weak-minded for giving in to the bullies, he felt so much pain about the boy being bullied that he went out of his way to help the boy. He listened to the boy and even tried to help defend him against the bullies afterward.

Empathy is at the base of all of our morals and ethics. Empathy is at the heart of most religious teachings. Empathy helps us define what is fair and just. A famous primatologist and ethologist (or at least as famous as a primatologist and ethologist could possibly be), Frans de Waal, goes even further, calling empathy, "The glue that holds humanity together."

So how can you develop the skill and become more empathetic?

Putting yourself in other people's shoes is one way of developing empathy for people. Famously, George Orwell wanted to know what it was like to be homeless, so he actually lived on the streets for a while, which not only allowed him to become more empathetic to the inequality the homeless experienced, but also allowed him to develop friendships with the beggars he lived with. Others have visited services for religions other than their own to better empathize with the beliefs of other people. Still others have done one of the best things you could possibly do to build empathy: travel to foreign countries and see firsthand how other people live.

Overall, one of the keys to being more empathetic is to find commonalities between you and others. When you look at someone from a different country or a different religion or a different race and view them as different, it becomes harder to see yourself in them. On the other hand, when you can find a way to identify with someone, when you find commonalities with someone, it becomes significantly easier to empathize with them and put yourself in their shoes.

If you're trying to empathize more with a person, focus on the things that you have in common with them, not the things that make you different from them. If you're a Christian trying to empathize with a Muslim, learn about all the similar beliefs between your religion and the Muslim religion, or simply focus on the fact that you both love Marvel superhero movies. If you're a straight person trying to empathize with a gay person, speak with them about dating issues that are similar to yours, or simply focus on the fact that you're both Chicago Cubs fans. If you're a sober person trying to empathize with an alcoholic, imagine trying to stop doing some little habit you're addicted to, like eating chocolate, or biting your fingernails; or simply focus on the fact that you are both great at Scrabble.

Although empathy is one of the hardest things to develop as you get older, it's also one of the things that defines your maturity. The good news is that empathy begets empathy. The more empathetic you are, the easier it becomes to empathize in the future, and the more the people around you become empathetic as well.

Develop and practice empathy. It will help you become less judgmental, and more understanding of what other people are going through.

#empathy

#empathyrules

#dountoothers

"Learning to stand in somebody else's shoes, to see through their eyes, that's how peace begins. Empathy is a quality of character that can change the world."

–President Barack Obama

DON'T FOLLOW ALL THE GREAT ADVICE IN THIS BOOK

Always keep working toward self-improvement, but set realistic goals. And when you fall short of your goals, give yourself a break.

There's a famous quote that says, "Those who ignore history are doomed to repeat it." Consider this Great Advice book you're reading to be a history book, whose purpose is to describe some of the mistakes that many other people before you have made (not necessarily me, of course, just many other people), and give you some Great Advice so that you're not doomed to repeat history by repeating those same mistakes.

People sure do make a lot of mistakes, and as a result, there's a lot of Great Advice to offer regarding how to avoid making those mistakes yourself.

If you agree with some of the Great Advice you've read about, and want to put it into effect in your own life, then make it a goal of yours. But realize that sometimes we don't reach our goals right away. Sometimes we don't reach our goals the first time we try. Sometimes we don't reach our goals for quite some time. And sometimes we don't ever reach our goals.

Even though this book is meant to help you learn from others' mistakes, it's inevitable that you probably won't take some of this Great Advice, and you'll have to make these mistakes yourself once. Or twice. Or maybe dozens of times. And that's OK. If it were so easy to read about some Great Advice and instantaneously change our ways by putting that advice into effect in our everyday lives, we would all do it right away.

So don't be unrealistic. Don't expect that you'll read this book and change all your ways overnight. And don't think you can do it in a week or a month or even a year. It's unlikely to be that easy. Sadly, it's not so easy to change our ways. It's not so easy to change our habits. And more importantly, nobody's perfect. We're all human. We all make mistakes.

Don't fall under the spell of something that social science researchers call "False Hope Syndrome." That's when you set a goal for yourself that is unrealistically high because you think that self-change is easy, and then, when reality smacks you in the face and you come to terms with the fact that changing is much harder than you expected, you lose hope, and abandon your goal.

When a character in a movie who is out of shape finally decides to change and get fit, they do so in a sixty-second montage of eating healthy and exercising, and then after sixty seconds, poof! They're healthy and fit! But there are no montages in real life. In real life, when you set a goal like that, you're in for months of hard work, sweat, hunger, sore muscles, avoiding food you love, and lots of sacrifice. And if you're not prepared for how hard the road ahead of you is, the first time you're offered a big hunk of cake and eat it, you'll get upset about the failure, lose all hope, and give up your goal. That's False Hope Syndrome.

The cure for False Hope Syndrome? Set big goals, but make sure the goals are still realistic, attainable goals. More importantly, give yourself a break. Don't feel guilty about not being perfect. Don't have negative thoughts about your inability to change. And most importantly, don't give up.

Strive for self-improvement, because it's generally good practice to always try to keep growing and bettering ourselves. But if you fall short of your goals, be happy with where you're at, and with the person you already are.

#greatadvicegoals

#giveyourselfabreak

#notperfect

#keepgrowing

"Set your goals high enough to inspire you, and low enough to encourage you."

–Unknown

DON'T GROW UP TOO FAST

Be happy with where you are in life, and don't be in such a hurry to do adult things like drinking, smoking, vaping, drugs, and sex.

You might sometimes look at your parents, and other adults, and get a little jealous of their independence, their money, their privacy, or their ability to do whatever they want without asking somebody's permission. It's like they're living in their own little paradise of freedom, right? Oh, to be an adult! You just can't wait to grow up.

Well I've got a little secret to share with you. You may be jealous of adults because of all those things they have, but the dirty little secret you don't know is...

Adults are jealous of you.

That's right! You live your whole teenage life wishing you were older, so you can "start your real life" and have all the benefits of being an adult, but then when you actually become an adult, you finally realize how good you had it when you were a teenager. One of the best, but most underappreciated, things about being a teen is that you don't have any "adult" problems (hopefully).

"But teens have big problems!" That's true. Very true. I haven't yet met a teen that doesn't have problems and drama in their life, and I haven't yet met a teen that doesn't think their problems and drama are just as bad as "adult" problems. But believe it or not, your problems will only get bigger and more serious as you get older.

Adults often have to deal with money, taxes, bosses, politics, war, the economy, crime, protecting their kids, providing for their kids, taking care of their parents, unwanted pregnancies, sexually transmitted diseases, being overweight, being unhealthy, death, career dissatisfaction, alcoholism, drug addiction, smoking, cancer, depression, and worst of all, figuring out who the hell Lizzo is.

Unfortunately, it's true that some teenagers have some of those adult problems as well, even though, in an ideal world, they shouldn't. But it should be the goal of every teen (and every parent) to reduce the number of "adult" problems they have to deal with. And one of the best ways to reduce the number of problems you're exposed to is...

Don't grow up too fast.

Don't take on those problems earlier than you have to. Don't do anything to cause those problems to arrive any earlier than they have to. And the top few things you might consider doing that would make those adult problems arrive earlier than they have to are drinking, smoking, vaping, doing drugs, and having sex.

Making a bad choice when dealing with any one of those things could easily change, or even ruin, your life in an instant. However, I should note that four of those things (drinking, smoking, vaping, and doing drugs) are considered "vices" that are generally bad for you at any age and are usually indicators of other problems in your life, while the remaining one, sex, is a normal, healthy, completely human activity that you'll probably partake in at some point in your life, when the time is right. As a result, let's table discussion of the good stuff, like sex, and just focus on the stuff that's bad for you, like drinking, smoking, vaping, and drugs.

It's true that a lot of teens, and even more adults, drink alcohol. And many smoke, vape, or use drugs too. But why? Why do people take part in activities that are so dangerous and destructive to themselves? Anybody who does take part in these activities is likely to reply, "Because it's fun and relaxing and takes away my stress."

But for a lot of those people, when they say it's "relaxing" or "takes away my stress," what they're really saying is, "It stops me from thinking about my problems." You should realize that the desire or need you feel to drink, smoke, vape, or do drugs as a teen is likely driven by a desire to ignore, dull, minimize, or avoid your problems. It's likely driven by a desire to escape and get away from thinking about your problems in order to relax.

And guess what. It works! It's probably true that drinking, smoking, vaping, and doing drugs might relax you for a few minutes or hours while you're doing them, and help you to escape for a few moments from thinking about, or even obsessing about, your problems. But (and this is a big "but") you've probably heard that, with any drug that gives you a relaxing "high" for a few moments, afterward comes a longer and stronger "crash" down low. So while your thoughts about your problems might go away during the high, all your problems come rushing back with a vengeance during the following crash, and remain there afterward, even worse than when you started. And to make matters even worse, the more often you get drunk or high, the longer and stronger the subsequent crash.

That's why it's important that you know that drinking, smoking, vaping, and doing drugs do not solve any of your problems, but rather, they hide them for a few hours, and then they multiply those problems and make them ten times worse for many hours. They turn your "teen" problems like bad grades, loneliness, tough breakups, being bullied, or mean parents into "adult" problems like alcoholism, addiction, mental illness, depression, suicidal thoughts, overdoses, crime, and sometimes, death.

Before you decide to grow up too fast and risk turning your teen problems into adult problems, try to solve your problems without drinking, smoking, vaping, or drugs. There are many better alternative methods, like meditation, listening to music, exercising, singing, dancing, sports, talking to your parents, talking to your friends, talking to a coach, talking to your teachers, or if things are really bad, talking to a professional therapist, who can help you through your problems without starting a habit that is only going to make your problems worse and create new, significantly bigger ones.

Don't drink, smoke, vape, or use drugs while you're a teenager. It'll only make your problems worse.

If you have problems that require professional help, email us at help@greatadvicegroup.com and we'll find a professional therapist to help you.

#dontgrowuptoofast

#nodrinkingnodrugs

#novaping

#livecleanteen

"Drugs take you to hell, disguised as heaven."

–Donald Lynn Frost

IF YOU DECIDE TO GROW UP FAST, DO IT WISELY

It's not a great idea to drink, smoke, vape, or do drugs as a teen, but if you're going to do it, make sure you do it smart.

As you now know from my previous piece of Great Advice, it doesn't make a lot of sense to ever start drinking, smoking, vaping, or doing drugs, *especially* while you're a teen. Let's call that Great Advice Plan A.

But Great Advice Plan A is not necessarily realistic advice for many teenagers. You might be thinking, *Every adult I know drinks, lots of kids at school drink, so it's crazy to advise me not to drink at all.* And it's true that about 86 percent of people drink alcohol, so telling some teens not to drink alcohol seems futile. If you've already decided that you'd like to try those things, then let me offer you what I think is a realistic, middle ground plan for you—what we'll call, Great Advice Plan B.

For Great Advice Plan B, I'll offer you a quick rule of thumb to live by whenever you're considering trying some new "adult" thing:

Wait a while. Wait a year.

From the day you decide you'd like to try one of those "adult" things, wait one more year before actually trying it. A year is a good waiting period to turn something that you "think you might be ready to try" into something that you "definitely are ready to try," or to figure out that you actually don't want to try it at all. Plus, waiting a year proves to yourself that you have willpower and self-control, which are important qualities you're certainly going to need if you want to avoid becoming addicted.

If waiting a year is still not specific enough and you want an actual age, then OK: wait until you're eighteen years old. That's when lots of teens leave home and either head to college on their own, or live independently outside of their parents' house. It's an age when teenagers start to become a bit more independent and mature enough to realize that they are now responsible for their own actions, and to realize the potentially serious consequences of those actions.

And if you want even more specifics about what you should be thinking about before making decisions like this, let me break it down for you in more detail.

Alcohol

Let's be honest and state that alcohol should qualify as a drug the same way we categorize other substances that affect your body chemistry as drugs. Alcohol just happens to be one of the most popular drugs in the world, perhaps only behind caffeine. Alcohol also happens to be one of the most destructive drugs commonly used, killing tens of thousands of people each year and ruining the lives of millions of alcoholics who become addicted.

So, if you are going to start drinking, make sure you don't set yourself on a path to becoming one of those casualties. Setting some hard and fast rules for yourself will allow you to drink alcohol, but will also give you some very well-defined metrics you can use to make sure that your drinking doesn't slowly and imperceptibly get out of your control. Here are my suggestions to "drink smart":

- Wait until you're eighteen. Or at least wait until your senior year of high school.
- Don't drink more than twice a month.
- Only drink on Friday or Saturday nights, never during the day.
- Don't drink to excess.
- If you do drink to excess and throw up, don't drink again for a month.
- If you have even one sip of alcohol, don't drive. (It's not worth trying to figure out if you're impaired.)
- If your driver has even one sip of alcohol, don't get in a car with them.
- If you set these (or similar) rules for yourself and consistently break them, ask for help.
- If you get drunk once a week or more, ask for help.
- If your friends say they're worried about your drinking, ask for help.

A special fact related to alcohol use among teens that is worth noting: The number one cause of death among teenagers is, by a huge factor, motor vehicle traffic accidents, which includes drunk driving. Remember this fact the next time you're about to get into a car with somebody who has been drinking, and then... don't get in the car.

The best alternative to driving with someone who has been drinking? Calling your parents to pick you up. As embarrassing as it might be for you to have them see you drunk, and as angry as they might be at you for getting drunk, they will secretly be happy that you gave them the chance to save your life, and proud that you made a smart, adult decision to call them. (And believe it or not, they too were once teens who might have gotten drunk once or twice.)

By the way, if you have a history of alcoholism in your family, I have different Great Advice for you: Treat yourself like you're already an alcoholic and never taste a drop of alcohol. Never. Not once. No exceptions. Don't tempt fate. Track your sobriety the same way alcoholics do by counting the days, months, and years since not having a drink (the day you were born, hopefully), and keep the streak going.

Smoking

Nicotine actually degrades the brain development of teens, and is harder to give up than heroin, so this is an easy one to give Great Advice for:

Don't try it. Don't do it. Ever.

It's a disgusting, unhealthy habit, with almost no benefits, and a boatload of negative effects. Only 14 percent of Americans smoke cigarettes, and I'm pretty sure 13.9 percent of them wish they had never started.

If you need to relax, there are about twenty other more effective ways of relaxing than becoming addicted to nicotine. Try meditation, listening to music, exercising, singing, dancing, sports, games, reading, making art, or dozens of other ways. Check out each and every one of those consequence-free methods before you try smoking. And if you're already addicted to smoking, get help immediately to break the habit before it gets even worse.

Vaping

Just as cigarettes have become significantly less popular among teenagers, vaping has become significantly more popular. Since the most common substance to vape is nicotine (or a drug that's even worse), for most teenagers my Great Advice for vaping is identical to my Great Advice for smoking. Don't do it. Ever. It's almost as bad as cigarettes, and possibly even more dangerous in many ways, since vaping also means you may be ingesting propylene glycol (which is used to make antifreeze and paint solvents), acrolein (which is used to kill weeds and causes permanent lung damage), and benzene (which is one of the primary substances found in car exhaust). If you're thinking of trying vaping, just picture yourself inhaling a mixture of antifreeze, paint solvents, and weed killer out of the tailpipe of a car. Yummy!

After all that, if you somehow, inexplicably, still decide you want to vape, set some "vape smart" rules for yourself so you don't end up getting addicted or getting hurt:

- Wait until you are eighteen, or your senior year in high school.
- Don't vape more than twice a month.
- Only vape on weekends.
- Only buy cartridges from reputable stores, never from individuals. (Really dangerous chemicals are sometimes added to cartridges bought off the street.)
- Only vape your own cartridges that you bought yourself, never somebody else's.
- If you find yourself breaking the rules you've set for yourself, ask for help.

Drugs

Teenagers are too young to be experimenting with drugs. So don't do drugs.

Drugs aren't a great idea for adults either, by the way. So don't do drugs even when you get older.

With that said, if you do decide to do drugs once you're older, don't ever do any exceptionally dangerous drugs such as heroin, methamphetamine, crack, cocaine, or opioids. In case you haven't heard, trying any one of these drugs just one time can begin an amazingly powerful addiction. So powerful, in fact, that an addiction to any one of these drugs is almost certain to ruin your life, or even end it. You may have noticed that you've probably heard exactly zero stories of a person who tried meth only once. That's because there's no such thing. If you try meth once, you've probably just become instantly addicted. And if you want to see what you will look like in the future after trying meth, just google "Meth before and after." (Spoiler alert: you'll look like a real-life zombie.) Stay away from all these highly addictive drugs at all costs.

One notable exception to the drugs above that should be mentioned is marijuana. Not so long ago, marijuana was lumped in with all the other dangerous drugs out there. Lately though, it seems like marijuana is being put in a class by itself, with several states having legalized it, and more than half of Americans having tried it. Teen use of marijuana seems to be growing, with more than 20 percent of teens having tried it.

Marijuana is still a drug though, and a dangerous one at that. And surprisingly to most teens, science has proven that marijuana is actually MORE dangerous for teens than it is for adults, because your brain is still developing. Teenage use of marijuana is tied to mental illness, depression, and a whole bunch of other not so great outcomes. The risks of long-term damage from marijuana usage aren't nearly as great once you turn eighteen, so think long and hard before giving it a try while you're still a younger teen.

If you're willing to ignore all those great reasons not to try marijuana as a teen, I recommend you set some rules for yourself similar to the rules around alcohol:

- Wait until you're eighteen to reduce the chances of long-term damage to your brain. Or at least wait until your senior year of high school.
- Don't use marijuana more than twice a month.
- Only use it on Friday or Saturday nights, never during the day.
- Don't use too much marijuana at once.
- If you use even a little, don't even think of driving.
- If you consistently break your rules, ask for help.
- If you use marijuana once a week or more, ask for help.
- If your friends say they're worried about your marijuana use, ask for help.

As a reminder, I strongly recommend you go with Great Advice Plan A and completely avoid most of these vices, or at least wait until you're an adult to try them. If you feel like you really want to try one of them, before you do, please talk to an adult or a friend about whatever problems might be pushing you toward that decision. And then if you still decide to start drinking, smoking, vaping, or using marijuana while you're still a teenager, be as responsible as you can possibly be by setting some ground rules around your usage like the ones recommended above and stick religiously to those rules.

Above all, if you start drinking, smoking, vaping, or using marijuana, make sure you are always in control of your usage of it, rather than the other way around.

#waitayear

#waitbeforeyouvape

#drinksmart

*"You get to
make your own
choices, but
you do not get
to choose your
consequences."*

–Unknown

DECIDE FOR YOURSELF WHEN YOU'RE READY TO HAVE SEX

Listen to all the opinions you want, but in the end, you have to decide for yourself when you're ready to have sex.

After drinking, smoking, vaping, and doing drugs, the next biggest "adult" decision that teens typically feel like they have to make is about sex. More specifically, "Should I have sex?"

But the "Should I have sex?" question is a really unique, personal decision that is dependent on your particular background, how you were raised, what your values are, what stage you and your body are in, and many other factors.

And it's an important decision, primarily because having sex just one time could lead to some lifelong consequences. And those lifelong consequences are not just limited to having to take care of a human being for the next eighteen years of your life. These consequences also include the possibility of catching a sexually transmitted disease (STD) in the form of a bacteria or virus that could give you lifelong sores or warts on your genitals, cause you to become infertile, give you brain damage, destroy your liver, give you cancer, or kill you. Over one million people catch an STD every day! Nothing like a bunch of warts on your genitals to remind you of that one night of great sex you had decades earlier, huh?

While it's hard to offer specific, exact advice about sex that is right for everyone, here are a few things I think we should all agree upon: Almost everyone in the world has sex. Both of your parents definitely had sex. Sex between two consenting people is usually a fun and enjoyable experience, to put it mildly. And despite what some cultures and religions sometimes put forth, there's absolutely nothing wrong, dirty, immoral, or embarrassing about consensual sex.

So the big question on everyone's mind then isn't really, "Should I have sex?" The answer to that question, for almost everyone in the world, is a huge, resounding "Yes!" The actual big question that is really at the heart of this is, "When should I start having sex?"

It's an important decision, for sure. But before I tell you how to make that decision, let me first tell you how NOT to make that decision:

Don't make that decision by allowing somebody else to make that decision for you.

First and foremost on the list of people who should not decide for you when you should start having sex is your potential sexual partner. While I'm sure you care about their feelings and want to make them happy, it's not their feelings that you're responsible for. It's your own feelings. And while you surely want to make them happy, it shouldn't make them happy if they're pushing you into doing something before you're really ready to do it. Don't let anybody pressure you, push you, guilt you, convince you, cajole you, or otherwise force you into having sex before you're ready. If you're making a major decision about sex, it doesn't matter that your partner is ready, only whether or not *you* are ready. And if you're in a relationship with somebody who is putting pressure on you to have sex with them before you're ready, it's a relationship you should strongly consider leaving. A partner who puts sexual pressure on you is a selfish partner, and they're selfish in the single most important area of life where it's important NOT to be selfish, and that's not typically the type of partner that is good to be with.

There are other people who also should not decide for you when to start having sex (even though they may THINK they should have a say in the matter): your parents, your friends, your religious leaders, and lots of others. Feel free to listen to your parents' opinions on the subject, and feel free to learn about what your religion teaches you to do, and feel free to get your friends' opinions on whether they think you're ready or not. But the decision of when to start having sex is a personal one, and ultimately, the decision is yours and yours alone to make. So how do you best make that decision? The best way to decide when you're ready to have sex is:

When your heart and your brain tell you that you're ready to have sex.

It's your heart and your brain that are best qualified to advise you on when you're ready to have sex. Your heart because it will help advise you on whether or not you're feeling close enough with somebody to connect with them in a way that involves a lot of different emotions, chief among them love, but also sometimes lust, desire, excitement, and fun. And your brain because it will help advise you on how wise it is to put yourself in an "adult" situation that has the possibility of leaving you with some lifelong consequences.

If your heart and brain tell you to wait until you're married, then you should wait until you're married. If your heart and brain tell you to wait until you're 17.4 years old (the average age people lose their virginity in the United States), then wait until you're 17.4 years old. If your heart and brain tell you to wait until you meet somebody you really love, no matter what age at which that happens, then wait until you meet somebody you really love. And if your heart and brain tell you to wait until you meet somebody who is really attractive that you kinda like, then wait until you meet somebody who is really attractive that you kinda like. (I'm not a big fan of this last one, but as I mentioned, it doesn't matter what MY heart and brain tell me, it matters what YOUR heart and brain tell you.)

Listen to all the opinions you want, but in the end, listen to your heart. Listen to your brain. And then decide for yourself when you're ready to have sex.

#waituntilyouareready

#listentoyourheartandbrain

#iwilldecideformyselfthankyou

#thedecisionisminealone

"Cinderella lost her slipper, not her virginity. You don't need to have sex to find your prince."

–Unknown

REMAIN A CONDOM VIRGIN

If you're going to have sex, remain a "condom virgin." Make sure you use a condom every time, all the time.

Sure, it might be difficult to decide when you're ready to have sex. But when you actually do decide you're ready to have sex, the one thing that absolutely shouldn't be a difficult decision for you is to make sure that all the sex you have is safe sex.

Safe sex means sex that is safe from catching a sexually transmitted disease from your partner, and sex that is safe from creating an unwanted pregnancy.

More specifically:

- Safe sex means, if you're a woman, you talk with your doctor about birth control before you have sex for the first time. If you don't want your parents to know about it, go to the doctor with a friend, or just go alone. But go.

- Safe sex means you take personal responsibility for birth control, and don't trust that your partner will take care of it. That means you make sure that you or your partner uses a condom. Every time. All the time.

- Safe sex means that, if you're a woman, you also use a second form of birth control like the pill, or an IUD. Condoms are only 99 percent effective, which sounds pretty good, up until you realize that if you were to have sex 100 times, the condom is going to fail one of those times.

- Safe sex means that you always assume your partner has an STD, and you always protect yourself from getting an STD by using a condom. Every time. All the time.

- Safe sex means you use a condom even if your partner says they were just tested by their doctor for STDs, or says they're on birth control, or says they promise they'll pull out in time, or says they promise they just want to try it for a second without a condom, or it's "only" oral or anal sex. You use a condom. Every time. All the time. No exceptions. Not even for a second.

- Safe sex means you take similar precautions even if you're in a same-sex relationship. While you're obviously off the hook when it comes to protecting against unwanted pregnancies, you're still on the hook for protecting against STDs. You just might need to substitute "dental dam" for "condom" as necessary.

Why do you have to be so careful to use a condom every time, all the time, even if your partner tested clean for STDs? Very simply, sometimes people have been known to cheat on or lie to their sexual partners. Obviously, YOUR partner would never do such a thing, but some would. And if your "clean" sexual partner has sex with somebody with an STD, that someone gives it to your partner, who gives it to you! Sharing is caring, right?!

And why do you have to be so careful to use a condom every time, all the time, even if your partner says they're on birth control or will pull out? Well, sometimes a woman forgets to take their pill. Sometimes a man forgets to pull out (not to mention it's not a very effective birth control strategy anyway). Sometimes people say they're on birth control when they're really not. It happens. So don't leave things to chance. And say it with me...

Use a condom. Every time. All the time.

And by using a condom every time, all the time, there's a nice little added benefit which is catching on with teens and adults alike. Not so long ago, it was very common for people to remain virgins until they were married. Your virginity, it was said, was a "special gift" that you only gave to your spouse.

Today, people are having sex earlier in life and getting married later in life, and it's pretty clear that "saving your virginity for marriage" isn't nearly as common as it used to be. But there's a nice idea gaining steam that is not only really smart, but also a great alternative for saving your virginity for marriage: saving your "condom virginity" for marriage.

What does it mean to be a condom virgin? Being a condom virgin simply means that you've never had sex without a condom. Being a condom virgin means you've used a condom every time, all the time. And when/if you get married, or meet that somebody who is extra special, you still have something special you can share with them on your wedding night, just like in the old days. Traditions die hard!

If you're going to have sex, make sure you use a condom. Every time. All the time.

#condomeverytimeallthetime

#everytimeallthetime

#condomvirgin

"If you think seven years of bad luck are too much for breaking a mirror, try breaking a condom."

–Unknown

COMPARE YOURSELF TO ONLY ONE PERSON

Comparing yourself to others is a waste of energy. The only valuable person to compare yourself to is Yesterday Me.

Most teens find themselves competing and comparing themselves constantly to those who are closest to them. For lots of teens, that means they compare themselves to their siblings, their parents, their friends, their classmates, their community, and sometimes even Jay-Z or Beyoncé.

When my good friend Archimedes Clutterbuck was a kid, he loved Trivial Pursuit. And he found that he was constantly comparing his trivia knowledge to that of his two sisters. When comparing himself to his older sister, this meant he was always falling short because of his disadvantage in age. And when comparing himself to his younger sister, this meant he was always coming out ahead because of his advantage in age. And eventually he realized the comparisons were really all just a façade.

He recognized that whether he came out ahead or behind was determined not by his actual knowledge of trivia, but by who he compared himself to. And that was somewhat arbitrary. Eventually, he decided to play it safe and just compare himself to the four-year-old girl across the street, which meant that he always came out ahead on everything.

What's the point of comparing yourself to somebody else? Is it to determine how good or bad you're doing at something? If so, that's a flawed comparison. It's less a measure of your skill, and more a measure of who you decide to compare yourself to.

There are 7.8 billion people in the world today. Why would you choose to judge yourself only in comparison to those who live in the same house as you? Or to those who are in the same classroom as you? Or to those who are in the same school as you?

Let's say that, compared to your best friend, you're the fastest at running the 100-meter dash. Congratulations! And let's say that, compared to all your classmates at school, you are still the fastest at running the 100-meter dash. You're amazing, you little speed demon!

But as you expand your comparison to different groups, eventually you'll find that you're no longer the fastest anymore, even though you're still just as fast as you were before. There might be a kid in another school district who runs faster than you, or a kid in the next county who runs faster than you, or a kid who lives in a different part of the state who runs faster than you. You don't feel so fast anymore, huh?

Unless you've won the gold medal for the 100-meter dash at the Olympics, there's always going to be somebody on this planet who runs faster than you. And on the flip side of the coin, there's always going to be somebody on the planet who runs slower than you.

Comparing yourself to others will either give you a false sense of security, or worse, give you a false sense of inferiority. And I'll give you one guess to tell me if most teenagers are more likely to compare themselves to somebody that makes them feel superior, or inferior. If you said teens are more likely to compare themselves to somebody that makes them feel superior, then you are absolutely, 100 percent... living on some other planet.

And so the point is, rather than compare yourself to somebody that's going to make you feel bad (or good) about yourself, don't waste a second comparing yourself to others at all. It's not productive, it's not informative, and it's not actionable. Most of the time, it's simply destructive.

"But if I don't ever compare myself to anybody," you might say, "then I don't have any incentive to push myself to get better." Good point! There's actually some truth to that. As a result, I suggest you make one big exception to the "no comparisons to others" rule.

The only person you actually should compare yourself to on a regular basis is somebody you should refer to as "Yesterday Me." If Yesterday Me ran the 100-meter dash in fifteen seconds, then it makes sense for Today Me to compare yourself to Yesterday Me and aim to finish in fourteen seconds. Comparing yourself to Yesterday Me makes sense, because it's the one person in the entire world for whom you know it's a fair comparison.

Otherwise, you risk thinking you're the best or worst at something, not because you actually are the best or worst at that thing, but only because you're the best or worst at something as compared to some tiny percentage of the population. And that means nothing.

Don't compare yourself to others. Just compare yourself to Yesterday Me.

#yesterdayme

#todaymevsyesterdayme

#Ibeatyesterdayme

"If you continuously compete with others you become bitter, but if you continuously compete with yourself you become better."

–Unknown

GREAT ADVICE #25

TAKE ACTION, RIGHT NOW

It's time to stop reading and start doing. Pick a piece of Great Advice and take action on it. Right now.

This is the most important piece of Great Advice in the whole book. The greatest of the Great Advice, you might say. But it's also the hardest advice for most people to take.

You probably have the best of intentions. You want to do lots of new things to improve yourself, improve your life, and improve the lives of others. Hopefully, that's one of the reasons you're reading this book. But I'm sure there are lots and lots of distractions in your life: television, social media, memes, music, video games, friends, school, hobbies, parents, siblings, movies, sports, homework, and more memes. Gotta have those memes!

Some of these distractions are valuable and important distractions. Obviously, spending time on homework is important. Spending time with friends is important. Spending SOME time relaxing with television or social media or yes, even memes, is good to recharge the batteries. But all these distractions get in the way of the one thing you should do that may be even more important:

Take action.

You surely have goals you're trying to reach. Things you're trying to accomplish. Some are small goals, and some are larger, more time-consuming goals. But almost anything you want to get done first requires that you stop procrastinating, stand up, and actually...

Take action.

Pablo Picasso said, "Action is the foundational key to all success." Thomas Edison said, "Genius is 1 percent inspiration and 99 percent perspiration." Nike said, "Just Do It." Lao-Tzu said, "The journey of a thousand miles begins with a single step." They all have the right idea. Having the right intention and mindset means absolutely nothing until you start to...

Take action.

This book can inspire you. I hope it has. But realize that reading this book and imagining yourself taking all this advice is not actually changing your life. It feels like you've changed, but that's just an illusion. If you just read a piece of great advice in this book, smile, nod your head and say, "Yeah, that's great advice; I'm going to do that," but then never actually do it, you're in no better shape than you were before you picked up this book. You've wasted a lot of time inspiring yourself to... do nothing. To actually change, you have to move past reading and thinking about all my Great Advice, and actually...

Take action.

Don't let yourself be categorized as one of those "all talk, no action" people. Instead, make sure you're a "no talk, all action" type of person. Often times, the difference between most people and the people who get things done and accomplish great things in this world is not smarts, creativity, or connections. It's taking action, and continuing every day to take action, until that action becomes a habit.

If you don't take this particular piece of Great Advice, all the other pieces of Great Advice mean nothing. How can you inspire yourself to actually take action? How can you make sure that, when you wake up tomorrow, you can look back on today and say, "I'm so glad I took action yesterday!" Well, there's only one surefire way I know to make sure that happens. And that is...

Take action. Right now.

That's right. Right now. Before you even finish reading this last piece of Great Advice, go flip through the book again, pick the one particular piece of Great Advice that you're most passionate about integrating into your life, and figure out a way to take action on it right now.

For instance, let's say that the Great Advice that spoke to you the most was Great Advice #13, "You Will Become Your Friends," which encourages you to choose your friends wisely and make new friends if your current friends aren't the ideal role models. You might decide to take action by making a list of five people that would be good friends to have because they're acting the way that you would like to act, and living their life the way you would like to live your life. You might even decide to REALLY take action to build a relationship by calling or texting one of those people with some excuse to reach out, or just to say hello.

Or in another example, let's say that the Great Advice that you were most passionate about was Great Advice #7, "Be a Creator, Not a Consumer," which encourages you to stop watching videos and spending time on social media, and start creating things that interest you. If programming is your thing, you might decide to write down a plan for that phone app you always wanted to create, and maybe even start writing the first one hundred lines of code for it.

Regardless, take the time to review the book now and find just one piece of Great Advice that speaks to you. Then take action in some way. Right now.

Go. Flip through the book. I'll wait.

Something tells me you're still reading this, but haven't actually taken action and flipped through the book to find something to take action on. You don't think I'm serious? Well, to inspire you to take action, I'm ending the book right here, right now, so you've got nothing to lose by finding something to take action on right now.

Thanks for reading! I hope you enjoyed the book.

OK, I lied. You got me.

I'm sorry about that. But did you actually take action on one of your favorite pieces of Great Advice? I hope so. The hard part in creating a new habit is just getting started, but once you do, the momentum kicks in and you're much more likely to remain motivated. So get started! Get moving! Get going!

Take action.

Stop planning, and...

Take action.

Stop thinking, and...

Take action.

Stop worrying, and...

Take action.

Stop preparing, and...

Take action.

Stop talking, and...

Take action.

Do it.

Take Action. Right now.

#takeaction

#takeactionnow

#takeactionrightnow

"Well done is better than well said."

–Benjamin Franklin

Help an Author (and One Hundred Million Other People)

At the beginning of this book, I described how I wrote the first version of *Great Advice* with the goal of helping my four children navigate their teenage years. As my kids got older though, my mission slowly expanded. I started to find that my friends were coming to me for help with different issues in their own lives, and so my goal expanded to help them with some Great Advice tailored to them and their unique problems.

Then I read a quote I loved by a guy named Shep Hyken, who said, "Every interaction you have is an opportunity to make a positive impact on others." And so I expanded my mission to try to help each and every person with whom I had a conversation. I made an effort to offer a particularly helpful and pertinent piece of Great Advice to almost everyone I talked to, in the hopes of ensuring that they left our conversation feeling better than when they started talking with me.

But that wasn't enough. I decided to come up with a new mission. A bigger mission. An absurdly grandiose mission.

My new mission would be to help not just my kids, not just my friends, and not just the people I interacted with. No, my new mission would be to help just 1 percent of the population. I figure if one hundred other people try to do the same and help just 1 percent of the population, then the whole world is taken care of. So that means with the world population at just around 8 billion people, I only have to help about 80 million people. No problemo!

And while we're at it, if I'm going to help 80 million, I might as well just round it up to an even 100 million people.

And so… that's my new mission:

"Help 100 million people."

More specifically, "Help 100 million people with at least one piece of Great Advice that changes each person's life in a meaningful way." And if I can help some of those 100 million people with two, or maybe even three pieces of advice that change their life, even better!

And with that mission came the best way to reach those 100 million people: this book you're reading now. This book that was originally meant to help just my four kids, but now is meant to help 100 million more people. And if this book has helped you, you are now one of those 100 million people. Hopefully you've found at least one piece of advice in this book that will help you change your life in a meaningful way. If it was two pieces of advice, or three, or four, or more, I'd be even happier.

If I have actually helped you, will you please join me in my mission to help 100 million other people? The easiest way to do that is to simply spend forty-two seconds to leave a short review of this book right now. You can do so right now by going to:

greatadvicegroup.com/review2

I read each and every review written, so you have my sincere appreciation. Leaving a review right now is the easiest and most valuable way you can help play a role in bringing great advice to 100 million people. Thank you in advance for helping so many other people, and thank you for making it this far in the book.

But if you've come this far, maybe you're willing to come a little further, and join the amazing community of readers at:

greatadvicegroup.com/teens2

There's a lot you can do on the website, including:

- Read other people's opinions, and leave your own comments, about my Great Advice.
- Vote for your favorite pieces of Great Advice.
- Purchase other Great Advice books.
- Submit your own Great Advice (and maybe get it published in a future book!)
- Read new Great Advice submitted by other readers and vote on the best ones.
- Get the Top Ten Greatest Great Advice of All Time.
- Read stories about how other readers used Great Advice in their life, and submit your own stories.
- See sneak previews of our future Great Advice and sign up to get Advance Reader Copies of our future Great Advice books.
- Help us decide which Great Advice should be included in future Great Advice books.
- Ask questions or post problems that are in need of Great Advice, to be answered by our team of coaches.
- Sign up for one-on-one coaching sessions with a professional coach.

I want to thank you for spending a great deal of time reading this book with the hope and faith that you'd receive something valuable in return for your time. I sincerely hope you found my Great Advice to indeed be great, and I hope that you are able to put some of my Great Advice into action to change your life for the better, and get even happier than you are today.

Best Regards,

Marc

Win a New Great Advice Book for Free

I run giveaways for my loyal readers (and even my not-so-loyal readers) all the time. You can win a free Great Advice book of your choice, a one-one-one videoconference with me, an hour with one of our professional coaches, and lots more.

In order to get a chance to win, just go to:

greaatadvicegroup.com/giveaway2

TEAR THIS BOOK APART

I'm about to ask you to do something that's a bit unorthodox, especially coming from an author. Are you ready? Are you sitting down?

If you have a non-electronic, old-fashioned, old-school, antiquated version of this book (AKA a paper copy), I'd like you to tear it up into pieces.

Wait! Not yet! Let me explain first.

As you've read through the book, you've probably found some pieces of Great Advice that particularly resonated with you. (At least I certainly hope you did!) You might have also discovered some pieces of Great Advice that you thought would resonate with somebody close to you: a friend, a family member, a classmate, or maybe even your archenemy.

If so, I'd like you to go back to each piece of Great Advice that you thought somebody you know would connect with and write that person's name at the top of the relevant chapter title page. (If you're reading this electronically, you can simply highlight the chapter title and leave yourself a note.)

Next, I'd like you to tear one of those individual pieces of Great Advice out of the book (or cut it out if you're not a fan of those raggedy edges), and give it to that person who you thought might benefit from it. And when you give it to them, ask them, in turn, to write down SOMEBODY ELSE'S name right below their own, who they think might benefit from it, and give it to that person. And then . . . well, you get the pattern.

Doing so will create a bunch of positive effects:

1. You'll feel great about yourself for having given your friend something that you think will help them.

2. Your friend will benefit from a piece of Great Advice that was custom-picked just for them.

3. Your friend will feel great about themselves for having forwarded that piece of Great Advice to help THEIR friend.

4. The next person will benefit from a piece of Great Advice that was custom-picked just for them.

5. This will cause a chain reaction, and together, we'll all feel great about helping 100 million people with Great Advice.

By the way, if you decided to save a tree and you have an electronic version of this book, you can still participate and share some Great Advice with a friend. Just go to:

greatadvicegroup.com/share2

WHO IS THIS ARCHIMEDES CLUTTERBUCK GUY?

Yeah, I know I talk about my "good friend" Archimedes Clutterbuck a lot, but he's quite an interesting character. As I've mentioned before, he's definitely NOT me, but if you're interested in knowing exactly who this Archimedes Clutterbuck guy really is, I'm more than happy to tell you. If you want to get to know the REAL Archimedes Clutterbuck, go to:

greatadvicegroup.com/whoisarchie2

BONUS ADVICE

MORE GREAT ADVICE FOR TEENS FROM OTHER GREAT ADVICE BOOKS

There are many more pieces of Great Advice that will also be of interest to you as a teen that have appeared in other Great Advice books. I've included a few of the best ones here in this section. But if you want more Great Advice that would be perfect for teens, please email us at info@greatadvicegroup.com and we'll be happy to give you some Great Advice about which other books will help you.

GREAT ADVICE #1

———————————

FIGURE OUT HOW TO BE SUCCESSFUL

Figure out for yourself what it means to be successful, and remember that the things that make other people feel successful might not be the same things that make you feel successful.

If I were to ask you who the most successful people in the world are, what names first come to mind? The most popular answers I get to this question are Bill Gates, Jeff Bezos, and Warren Buffett.

Why do those people keep coming up more than any other? After all, there are lots of successful business people in the world who have built really successful companies that are helping lots of people live better lives. So why those three? The answer is probably obvious: money.

Those three people happen to be among the richest people in the world. They're at the top of the top of what we call "the 1 percent." And the way most people measure somebody's success is by how much money they have.

Here's the interesting thing though. If you're making more than about $32,000 a year, you are part of the 1 percent too. To be specific, you're part of the top 1 percent of income earners in the world. That means you're earning more than 7 billion other people. So does this make you feel successful? And if you're not making more than $32,000 a year, does that make you feel unsuccessful?

Maybe. Maybe not. But regardless, is money the only way of measuring success? Is money the best way of measuring success?

No, it isn't.

In fact, the best metric to measure success is not the amount of money you have, but rather, it's the amount of happiness you have. Happiness is the one thing we're all trying to maximize. Now it just so happens that most people believe the biggest driver of their happiness is how much money they have. But is it actually true that money really does drive happiness?

As it turns out, it isn't true. Money is not the biggest driver of happiness. Not by a longshot.

In the most recent rankings of the richest countries of the world, Qatar was ranked the highest in per capita income. But you may be surprised to learn that Qatar is only ranked 29th when it comes to happiness. On the other hand, Finland is ranked all the way down at number 24 when it comes to average per capita income. But Finland is also ranked as the happiest country in the world. So why isn't the richest country the happiest, and why isn't the happiest country the richest? (And more curiously, why is Finland so happy when they're also so cold?)

Even though most people directly tie money to happiness and success, when they are pressed on the issue, most of them quickly realize this isn't true. Don't believe me? I'm going to make you a deal, and I'd like to know if you would accept the offer.

I'll snap my fingers and make you an instant billionaire. You will have all the money you will ever need, a beautiful house, a huge yacht, a private jet, and most importantly, the latest iPhone. But... in the process, you'll lose contact with all your current friends, your spouse or significant other, your parents, your brothers and sisters, and your extended family members. You'll have all the money you want but you'll have no loved ones to share it with. Is that success to you?

I'm guessing it's not. And I'm guessing it's not because I happen to know that a lot of people who have a huge bank account, a huge house, and a huge yacht, also have huge therapy bills. And they have huge therapy bills because they realized, perhaps a bit too late, that their success wasn't only driven by money, and that they may have dropped the ball in other areas of their life in which they also measure their success and happiness.

There are lots of other ways to define success, other than how much money you have. One of the best illustrations of this I've heard is a story that my good friend Archimedes Clutterbuck told me the last time he went skiing. He took a lesson with a ski instructor who had been doing his job more than forty years. The instructor lived a pretty spartan, frugal life, living out of his van most of the year. But he also told Archimedes, "I'd rather live out of my van and ski every day out in nature than make ten times more money and be stuck inside at a desk all day." He measured his success not by how much money was in his bank account, but by how many days a year he was able to ski.

The things that make your friends think you're successful, the things that make your parents think you're successful, and the things that make your colleagues think you're successful, might not be the same things that make YOU feel successful. You're responsible for figuring out for yourself the things that will make you feel successful and the things that will bring you happiness.

And there are a huge variety of things that you might use to determine how successful you are: how many days you get to ski, how many close friends you have, how many people you make laugh, how many kids you have, how many countries you visit, how much time you spend with your significant other, how many lives you save, how many trees you plant, or how many people you feed.

So don't assume that money is the best measure of your success and happiness, because it probably isn't. Figure out for yourself what it means for you to be successful.

#findyourownsuccess

#moneyaintsuccess

#successishappiness

"Don't measure your success with someone else's ruler."

–Unknown

GREAT ADVICE #4

DON'T HAVE TOO MANY FRIENDS

Don't worry so much about how many friends you have. When it comes to friendship, it's all about quality, not quantity.

In our society, it seems like we're taught that more is always better. More money, more cars, more possessions, more power, more status, more everything! Obviously though, it's not exactly true, or even close to true. One area in particular that this rule doesn't apply is when it comes to friendships.

With friendships, more does not mean better.

Lots of people aspire to be popular. Popular people have plenty of friends and admirers who want to spend time with them. It's like being a bit of a local celebrity. And as a result, people often go out of their way to accumulate a lot of friends. Even our social media tracks how many "friends" or "followers" we have, even though most of them can't really be considered friends at all, just acquaintances. Or even strangers.

Creating new friendships is obviously a really good thing to do. And it seems like the more friendships we create, the better. Especially in college, where the opportunities to meet new people and create friendships are ten times more abundant than what you experience in the "real world," you might naturally have the tendency to be so overwhelmed and excited by all the new people you meet, that you end up trying to maintain every single one of those friendships. In short, you feel like you want to be friends with everyone you meet.

But there's a big problem with having a lot of friends. You end up spreading yourself really, really thin. It takes a lot of time and effort to keep up with friendships, and the more friendships you try to keep up with, the more time and effort it takes. As a result, you end up with lots and lots of friends, but no close friends.

And close friends are what life is all about. Close friends are the ultimate goal.

Close friends are something more than just a friend. So much more. They make you a better person. They support you when times get tough. They listen to you. They're honest with you (whether you're right or wrong). They always have your back (whether you're right or wrong). They make you laugh. They make you feel better. They help you live longer. They help you chill out. They keep you humble. They forgive you. They trust you. They truly care about you.

It's not easy to find a close friend. In fact, if you're lucky enough to find even two or three close friends in your lifetime, I think you're doing pretty darn well. It's a challenge to find a close friend primarily because of all the time it takes to find someone you really connect with, and to build enough trust with them to move the friendship to the next level.

In fact, scientists have studied friendship and figured out about how long it takes to develop a friend and a close friend. Short answer: a lot of time. They found that it takes, on average, 164 hours of time together for an acquaintance to become a friend. And to make a good friend, it takes, on average, spending 219 hours together! So obviously, the more people you're acquaintances or friends with, the harder it is to spend the 219 hours it takes to really connect and bond to create a "close friend."

I should be clear that having some close friends still doesn't preclude you from having lots of other friends. The key is to make sure that you're spending extra time—quality, meaningful time—with your close friends. Because if you're trying to connect closely with too many people at once, you end up not connecting closely with anybody at all. In other words, finding and developing close friends is a matter of depth over breadth. Quality over quantity.

Don't worry so much about how many friends you have. Focus on developing your relationships with your close friends by spending quality time with them.

#qualityoverquantity

#depthoverbreadth

#bestiesforever

"Wishing to be friends is quick work, but friendship is a slow ripening fruit."

–Aristotle

Great Advice #2

Treat Your Car Like a Gun

Driving a car is the most dangerous thing you are ever likely to do, so be as careful driving as you would be if you were holding a gun in your hand.

Soon, self-driving cars will be ubiquitous. But until that day comes, this Great Advice has the potential to change your life more than almost any other piece of advice I could give you.

Since the day you were born, the chances of you accidentally killing yourself were probably pretty small. Sure, there was that time you choked trying to swallow that Lego piece, and that time you ran out into the street to retrieve your soccer ball, and that time you rode down the hill on your bike without any brakes, but somehow you survived. Maybe you survived with a skinned knee, or a broken leg, but you survived. Congratulations on making it this far!

Even as you grow older, unless you decide to join a gang (don't), make stupid parkour videos on top of skyscrapers (don't), or listen nonstop to Justin Bieber's music (definitely don't), your chances of living to a ripe old age are pretty good. But the minute you get your driver's license and sit behind the wheel of a car, the chances of you growing old go down quite a bit.

Most teens are so excited at the amount of independence that getting their driver's license offers them that they never stop to think about the unique situation they're now putting themselves in. When you drive a car, for the first time in your life, you are putting yourself in control of a machine that weighs several tons and can go a hundred miles an hour. For the first time in your life, you are putting yourself in control of a machine that can easily kill you.

Think of driving a car as the equivalent to holding a loaded gun in your hand. If I put a loaded gun in your hand, would you wave it around and try to spin it around your finger like the cowboys do on TV? (Please say no.) Or would you be really, really nervous and focus all of your attention on making sure you didn't drop that gun by mistake?

The problem is that, while it's easy to see a gun as a dangerous weapon because it's created to be used as one, it's hard to view a car that way. A car is supposed to give you the ability to get yourself wherever you want to go, whenever you want to go there. It's a machine designed to give you convenience, to give you independence, and to give you a way to get your fast food a few seconds earlier by using the drive-thru line. It's not a machine designed to kill people. But the numbers don't lie, and every day, a car does kill someone. Lots of people. In fact, historically, the number of annual automobile deaths in the United States has been much higher than the number of annual gun deaths. In other words, cars can be more dangerous than guns. And it's even worse for teenagers. Care to guess what the number one cause of death is among teenagers? If you said motor vehicle traffic accidents, you're right.

If you're already driving, or about to drive, you're probably already scared of getting in an accident and killing yourself, which would obviously be awful. (We'd all miss you dearly.) But there's something that should scare you even more: the possibility of your driving causing somebody else's death. If you're the type of person who would never consider picking up a gun and shooting somebody (and I hope that you are), realize that driving a car could result in the same consequences.

And those same consequences include you going to jail, because even when somebody inadvertently causes a car crash that results in somebody else's death, the law treats it similarly to how it would if you accidentally shot and killed somebody.

Soon after my good friend Archimedes Clutterbuck got his driver's license, he found himself driving down the highway on a sunny day, listening to the radio, without a care in the world. He was just about to miss the turnoff for his highway exit, so he quickly switched into the right lane going 60 miles an hour, a maneuver he had done hundreds of times before. But unlike the hundreds of times that he had done it before, this time, there was a motorcyclist in his blind spot. The side of Archie's car slammed into the motorcyclist, sending the motorcyclist flying off the side of the highway down an embankment. When Archimedes pulled off the road and got out of his car, he dreaded the thought of looking down the embankment at a dead body at the side of the road. A body of a man whose death he was responsible for.

Imagine yourself in that situation. Imagine living with the knowledge for the rest of your life that your one quick turn of the steering wheel—a simple, thoughtless action—killed a human being. And don't think it can't happen to you, because it most certainly can. Worldwide, it happens to more than 3,000 people every single day. And I guarantee you that every single one of those 3,000 people assumed that they'd never get in an accident and kill somebody (or themselves). Until they did.

If it does happen to you, you're in for a lifetime of asking yourself, "What if I had driven more carefully, or more slowly? Would that person still be alive?" But even if you had been driving as carefully and as slowly as humanly possible, and weren't in the least bit careless with your driving, does it even matter? You were still behind the wheel of a car that took somebody's life, whether it was your fault or not.

All of those thoughts and more went through Archimedes's head in the seconds between the crash and the moment he looked down to see the motorcyclist he had hit. But in what is literally the luckiest thing that has ever happened to Archimedes, the motorcyclist was fine, suffering only a broken finger. Unfortunately, as the motorcyclist displayed to Archie, it wasn't his middle finger that was broken.

When driving a car, you're making dozens of decisions every minute you're on the road. Given the hundreds or thousands of hours that you might drive over a lifetime, you need to fully appreciate that if just one of those decisions is made with a bit less care than the others, it has the potential to change your life, and somebody else's life, forever.

So when you get behind the wheel of a car, realize that driving safely requires the same amount of attention and care as if you were holding a loaded gun. Because in many ways, you are.

#acarisagun

#drivesafe

"Drive slow and enjoy the scenery. Drive fast and join the scenery."

–Douglas Horton

Great Advice #18

Have Deep,
Meaningful Conversations

The building blocks of creating close friendships are deep, meaningful conversations, so have as many of those conversations as possible.

Hopefully, I've already convinced you of the value in developing a few really close friends in your life. But that's easier said than done, isn't it? Finding a really close friend is something that is likely to happen only a handful of times in your life. It's rare to meet somebody you really click with. So how do you improve your chances or accelerate your meaningful friendships?

Well, I'm happy to report that if you're living on a college campus, especially if you're living in a dorm, you're in the perfect position to do just that.

Obviously, college already has a lot of things going for it: learning about interesting new things, living on your own for the first time, being challenged in ways you've never been challenged before, and of course, going deep into debt while paying obscenely high tuition prices. (OK, maybe that last one isn't so great.)

But one of the most valuable things that college has going for it is it's probably the first (and perhaps the last) time in your life when you are surrounded by an entire microcosm of people your age–fascinating and interesting people with completely different and diverse backgrounds, beliefs, and interests. Especially if you live in a dorm, most of your time is spent surrounded by your peers, without an adult in sight. Living in close quarters with so many young people creates an amazing environment to have some pretty special shared experiences. And those shared experiences typically cause some really close friendships to develop. And that is probably one of the most valuable things that college has going for it. Those shared experiences with friends. And those shared experiences with friends are exactly what turns close friendships at college into lifelong friendships throughout life.

These valuable shared experiences can be any number of different things. It might be going to school football games together, or acting crazy at a party together, or sneaking into a bar with fake IDs together, or eating your meals together in a dining hall, or simply watching your favorite TV show together. But one of the most valuable shared experiences you could possibly have at college also happens to be one of the simplest: just having a deep, meaningful conversation with other people.

Why are deep conversations so important and valuable? Science has actually studied this very question, and has proven that deep, meaningful conversations are strongly tied to happiness. They're tied to happiness for two main reasons. First, we human beings seem to be complicated creatures, and one of our most basic drives is to create meaning in our lives. Having meaningful conversations helps us do just that. Second, we human beings also seem to be very social creatures (even the introverts among us), and deep conversations help us to connect with others.

In fact, I mentioned earlier that scientists have found that you need to spend an average of 219 hours with another person to turn a friend into a truly close friend. However, those same scientists have figured out a sneaky way to artificially shorten the time it takes to develop a close friend: by having deep, meaningful conversations.

Deep conversations can take on many forms, and can be about many different topics. They can be about topics you all agree upon or topics you violently disagree on. Deep conversations can be about topics that make you uncomfortable or topics that you've discussed many times before. The only real requirement for a deep, meaningful conversation is that the topic is... deep and meaningful.

"This is some weather we're having, huh?" doesn't really help get you to the meaningful stuff. "What are your hopes and dreams in life?" gets you closer. "Why are those your hopes and dreams?" probably does the trick.

It's pretty easy to create deep, meaningful conversations with somebody, but here are a couple tricks to help you along the way:

- Be genuinely interested in learning more about the human being sitting across from you. That's generally enough to get a deep conversation going. Be inquisitive about things you never knew about them.

- Look for topics that you disagree on, but rather than becoming combative and trying to convince them of your point of view, probe and challenge them to find out why it is exactly that they hold that specific opinion. Try to be open-minded to their point of view, and ask how they'd respond to counterarguments.

- Ask personal questions, and volunteer your own personal thoughts and feelings as well. This requires a lot of vulnerability, but it will increase the amount of trust you build with somebody quickly.

- While somebody is telling you something interesting, focus less on how you're going to respond when they're done talking, and more on the substance of what it is they're saying. Long awkward pauses in a deep, meaningful conversation aren't really awkward at all, but rather an indication that things are deep and meaningful.

- Prepare a list of deep, meaningful conversation topics. There are entire books written just focused on deep, interesting questions, and ten times as many lists on the internet with similar conversation starters. Here are my favorite questions used by those scientists who found that deep conversations accelerate close friendships:

  - If you could choose anybody in the world as your dinner guest, who would it be?

  - For what in your life do you feel most grateful?

  - If you could change anything about the way you were raised, what would it be?

  - Is there something that you've dreamed of doing for a long time? Why haven't you done it?

  - What are your most treasured and your most terrible memories?

  - When did you last cry?

  - What does friendship mean to you?

Some of your most memorable times in college will be some of the amazing, deep, meaningful conversations you have with others sitting on the floor of your dorm room, or at a restaurant at one in the morning, or walking to class across the entire campus.

Deep, meaningful conversations will become the building blocks of some of your closest friendships throughout your life. So do what you can to have as many deep, meaningful conversations as possible.

#deepmeaningfulconversations

#deepconversationtopic

#talkdeeptome

"Good conversation is as stimulating as black coffee, and just as hard to sleep after."

–Anne Morrow Lindbergh

Great Advice #21

Fail on Your Way to Success

Failing to try is really the worst failure of all. So give up your fear of failing, and remember that failing is the most common path to success.

It feels great when you succeed. It kind of sucks when you fail. You would probably prefer to succeed rather than fail. I know I might be going out on a limb here, but I'm confident that's all true.

But don't worry so much about failing. I know you'd probably rather get a paper cut and pour lemon juice on it than to fail, but I'm here to convince you otherwise. (Besides, there's not much upside to getting a paper cut and pouring lemon juice on it, although I'm certain a video of you doing so would get about a billion views on YouTube).

Failure doesn't always have to be a bad thing. Failure doesn't even always have to mean that you failed. You can reframe and rethink every failure and mistake as something more positive, as just another step toward gaining more experience on your way to ultimate success.

Even more importantly, remember that, usually, failure is actually a success in disguise.

For instance, my good friend Archimedes Clutterbuck spent a lot of time and money to start a business repairing computers. He found many customers that needed their computers to be repaired, but unfortunately, he didn't have the knowledge he needed to do many of the repairs quickly, and his business eventually failed. Obviously, he wasn't so happy about that.

But in the course of that failure, he realized that, although he wasn't good at fixing computers, he was really great at finding customers that needed computer repairs. And as it turns out, there were lots of computer repair companies that needed help finding customers. So he started a new business that helps repair companies find customers, and that new business is an amazing success. And of course, he would've never realized that the market had a need for his service if he hadn't first started his repair business and failed at it. That's success disguised as failure!

But remember, failure can also be disguised as success. Imagine you set a goal to run a 5K race in less than sixty minutes, and on your very first try, you not only accomplish that goal, but you actually finish the race in thirty minutes. Congratulations! We're all very proud of you. Fantastic success!

But is that really a success? If your goal was to run the 5K in sixty minutes, and you actually ran it in thirty minutes the first time you tried, maybe you didn't set your sights high enough. Maybe running five kilometers in thirty minutes isn't such an amazing accomplishment after all. You might even say that, even though you succeeded at running a 5K race in less than an hour, maybe you failed by setting your goal so low to begin with.

Now it's certainly true that, when you set your sights really, really high, you're significantly increasing the chances that you're going to fail or make a mistake early on in the process. But that's fantastic! Don't treat it as a "failure," treat it as a sign that you've successfully challenged yourself to accomplish a lofty goal, and you've successfully discovered one way not to accomplish that goal.

With every additional "successful failure," you rule out yet another wrong way of doing it and get closer and closer to finding the right way.

In fact, if you've never failed at all, that in and of itself is one of the greatest failures of all. If you've never failed at something, then you've probably only set really safe and realistic goals for yourself. You've probably never really pushed yourself. Never really challenged yourself. Never really set the bar high enough.

Or even worse, maybe you've never failed because you just don't even try. Because you'd rather not attempt something at all than risk failing at it. Because your fear of failing is stronger than your drive to succeed.

Fear of failure is a really common problem for a lot of people, and I can tell you that it's one of the saddest problems to have. It's sad because it's a paralyzing fear, keeping you from accomplishing amazing things. Fear of failure guarantees that you won't fail, but it also guarantees that you won't succeed.

So give up your fear of failing! Failing to try is really the worst failure of all. Failing is not the end of the world, but rather, the most common path to success.

#failoften

#reframeyourfailure

#failureleadstosuccess

"It is impossible to live without failing at something, unless you live so cautiously that you might as well not have lived at all. In which case, you fail by default."

–J.K. Rowling

GREAT ADVICE #14

IF YOU DRINK A SIP, DON'T DRIVE

Use this all-or-nothing rule when driving, and don't ever make any exceptions to it.

Every 50 minutes, somebody in the United States dies in a car crash related to an alcohol-impaired driver. That's almost 30 people every day, 7 days a week, 365 days a year. That results in over 10,000 DUI related deaths every year. Even worse, there are over 100 million occurrences of driving under the influence (DUI) each year, but only about 1 million of them get caught and arrested.

Clearly, driving under the influence is a major problem, causing a lot of senseless deaths.

The blood alcohol concentration (BAC) limit in almost all areas of the country is .08 percent. So all you have to do is make sure you don't drive a car when your BAC is .08 percent or higher. But how do you know what your BAC is at?

The simplest solution is just to "feel" how drunk you are, and be honest with yourself about whether or not you feel competent to safely drive a car. It's a great solution! You're pretty in touch with your feelings, right?

Wrong. Nobody is really good at accurately identifying how drunk they are. I've seen many people struggling to stand up that thought they were just fine to drive home. I've also seen many people who seemed completely sober and competent to drive, but had a BAC of above .08 percent and still got arrested. So in the end, as solutions go, this "feel" how drunk you are approach is a pretty crappy one.

Luckily, there are more scientific ways of measuring your BAC. One of the simpler methods is to count how many drinks you have each hour, and remember that the average person can only have one drink per hour and still drive safely (with a "drink" being defined as one beer, one glass of wine, or one shot of hard alcohol). Great! Simple counting. You can count, right? Even when you're drunk!

Counting isn't the issue. You'll notice that I said "The average person" should only have one drink per hour. That's a big problem, because most of us aren't exactly average, and nobody really knows how the average person is defined. Once again, not a great way of solving the problem.

Thankfully, though, you can easily solve that problem by using a BAC app on your phone, which asks you to input the number of drinks you had, your height, weight, and gender, and then tells you your BAC estimate. Fantastic! You can simply download the app! Problem solved.

Problem not solved. The app tells you your BAC estimate, with the key word there being "estimate." Your BAC isn't just dependent upon how many drinks you had, your height, your weight, and your gender. Your BAC is also dependent upon your diet, your medical conditions, the kind of alcohol you drank, the food you ate, your psychological state, fatigue, your genetic makeup, and other unique individual characteristics. So unfortunately, the BAC calculator isn't really accurate enough.

Fortunately, there's another great solution out there. You can buy a smartphone breathalyzer attachment and measure your own BAC level. Great! All it takes is little bit of money! You've got enough money to buy a smartphone breathalyzer.

Sadly, portable breathalyzers just aren't that accurate either. And when life and death are on the line, you don't really want to leave things to a machine that isn't always accurate.

But I've got good news. You could really go all out and buy an expensive professional breathalyzer, the same kind that the police use. Those are actually accurate. Sure, it seems like a lot of money to spend, but it's worth it, right? And sure, it's a bit inconvenient and embarrassing to lug a breathalyzer with you to a party just to be able to drink and drive. But at long last, using a police breathalyzer will definitely make sure you're under the .08 percent BAC limit.

Except I've got some more bad news for you. Remember that .08 percent BAC limit I mentioned before? When you look at the fine print, you realize that .08 percent BAC is the limit for drivers who are 21 and older. If you're under twenty-one, then the legal BAC limit isn't .08 percent, it's .02 percent in most states. And that is such a low number that it's practically impossible to have a drink and still be below .02 percent. In fact, many states don't even bother with that, and set their legal BAC limit at .00 percent.

That's right. If even a drop of alcohol is detected in your blood, you're going to jail.

So what's a driver to do? If you're under twenty-one, how the heck are you supposed to know whether or not it's safe to drive? How long do you have to wait until the one drink you had leaves your bloodstream and gets you down below .02 percent BAC?

Fortunately, some brilliant scientists in Sweden have recently discovered a foolproof method of figuring out your blood alcohol concentration that's always 100 percent accurate. It doesn't require that you plug in your age, weight, height, gender, how much you ate, what you drank, how you feel, or any other information. It doesn't require that you carry an expensive machine and breathe into it and hope that it's accurate. Their scientifically proven method is amazingly simple, amazingly accurate, amazingly cheap, and it works every single time without fail. It's a bit complicated to understand, but let me walk you step by step through the method they devised and see if you can follow along:

Step 1: If you have a sip of alcohol, don't drive.

That's right. One sip, and you're done for the night. It's a simple method, and if you live by that one little rule religiously, you'll never have to worry what your BAC is. You'll never have to worry about getting arrested, thrown in jail, and losing your driver's license. And best of all, you'll never have to worry about being one of those people who drives while impaired and kills somebody.

You should realize that the stakes are already high enough when you're sober and you sit down in the driver's seat. Driving is already dangerous enough while completely unimpaired. If you drink, even a little, then you add to that already dangerous situation the fact that your driving isn't quite as good as it could be, and now you've got a really good recipe for somebody dying.

It isn't worth it.

Just commit to deciding at the beginning of the night, "Is this a drinking night, or is it a driving night?" If it's a drinking night, leave the car at home. And if you decide it's a driving night, but then you change your mind and have a drink, simply call a taxi, Uber, Lyft, your friend, your parent, or just walk home. It's always easy enough to go back and get your car the next day. All it costs you is some money for the rides, and a little bit of your time—both of which are worth it to avoid the chance of much, much worse consequences.

If you have even a sip of alcohol, don't drive. Set this as a simple all-or-nothing rule, and don't ever make any exceptions to it. It's not worth the risk of getting it wrong and possibly killing somebody.

#notonesip

#dontsipandrive

#onesipandyouredone

"Better to arrive sober and late than never."

–Unknown

GREAT ADVICE #10

HELP SOMEBODY

Give some of your time to help somebody less fortunate than yourself. If you give of yourself, you will inevitably get more than you expect.

There is a Chinese proverb that says: "If you want happiness for an hour, take a nap. If you want happiness for a day, go fishing. If you want happiness for a year, inherit a fortune. If you want happiness for a lifetime, help somebody."

In this day and age, we sum up the same sentiment with the phrase, "It's better to give than to receive."

Why is everyone so generous? What are people getting from giving?

As it turns out, a lot.

Scientists have given us compelling data to support the idea that one of the best ways to happiness is by giving to others and helping others. But there are a lot of ways to give and help.

The easiest way is to give your money. You can give your money to charities, non-profits, some stranger on a street corner, religious institutions, etc. And it feels good to take money that you worked really hard for, and give it to people who need it a bit more than you do.

But you know what feels even better?

Giving your time. As you may have learned by now, your time is significantly more valuable than your money.

If you've never spent the time to volunteer in a soup kitchen, or deliver meals to the homeless, or help volunteer in the oncology ward of a hospital, or given of your time to help others on a one-on-one basis, you should. The feeling you get after donating money is significantly different than the feeling you get after personally helping people truly in need, people significantly less fortunate than yourself.

Giving your money is great. But it's quick and impersonal. Giving your time allows you to see, meet, connect with, and build relationships with the people that you're helping. Obviously, it takes a bit more effort to give your time than your money. After all, you usually can't just show up at the hospital and ask to volunteer, you have to submit an application and probably get a bit of training. But there are simpler ways to give your time.

You probably pass a homeless person on the street every once in a while, right? It only takes about ten minutes to buy two sandwiches and sit and talk to them while you share a meal. You probably live somewhere near a retirement home, right? It only takes about twenty minutes to pass out a dozen roses to the residents, listen to their stories, and brighten their day.

You don't even have to leave your house to give your time. If you search for "Virtual Volunteer" you'll find dozens of websites like onlinevolunteering.org (run by the United Nations) and dosomething.org (tailored for young people to enact social change) that enable you to help people all over the world without ever getting up from your chair.

Whatever you decide to do, giving your time to help others has a bunch of really nice byproducts.

It will make you more empathetic to other people and their situations. No matter how much you read or watch about what it's like to be homeless, you can't possibly know and feel what a homeless person goes through without getting to know them personally and hearing their story.

It will make you more grateful for what you have. Keeping up with the Joneses is a real problem in our society, and you might be one of those people who constantly compares yourself to anybody who is better off than you. But sometimes, it's good to be with people less fortunate than yourself, simply to remind yourself how silly it is to think about and be anxious about some of the "first world problems" you have.

It will make you appreciate the real drivers of happiness. When you meet people less fortunate than yourself, you might realize something surprising. Often times, you'll find that many of these "less fortunate" people seem to be significantly happier than you'd expect, given their circumstances. You might even find that many of them are significantly happier than you are.

Think hard about this. If someone who sometimes struggles to meet their basic needs, like food and shelter, has such a positive attitude, and can be so happy with so little, perhaps they know something you don't. Perhaps the things you think will make you happy are not really the things that will actually make you happy.

And let me give you some additional Great Advice to help you supercharge the feeling you get from giving: *Keep it a secret*. Don't tell anybody that you gave money to the charity, or volunteered at the hospital, or bought a meal for the guy on the street corner, or helped serve food at the homeless shelter. Keep this one part of your life just for yourself.

Why? When you tell people you did something generous, you get the added benefit of feeling proud that people know that you did something generous. But you'll also find that, eventually, you start questioning, "Am I really doing this to be generous, or am I doing this just because it makes me feel good to know that people think I'm a generous person?"

Don't allow yourself to question your own motives. Keeping it a secret ensures that you never have to wonder why you're being generous. Keeping it a secret ensures that you know you're doing it not for yourself, but for others. And even though you don't get the buzz from people knowing what a great person you are, the fact that YOU know what a great person you are will make giving of your time ten times more valuable to you.

And if you've still got some "give" in you after all that, you can do even more. The Jewish Talmud recognizes eight different levels of giving. The highest level, the most noble, is not just to help somebody, but to help somebody to become self-sufficient. To invest the time to help them overcome not just their immediate challenges, but their long-term challenges, so that they can eventually stop needing help, and start helping others.

In other words, "Give a person a fish, and you feed them for a day. Teach a person to fish, and you feed them for a lifetime."

Admittedly, it's not easy to invest your time to selflessly help others. If you can spend even two hours a week (that's only 1 percent of your time) helping others, you're doing more than most people.

No matter how much time or money you spend, and no matter how you decide to do it, help somebody in some way. Give of yourself. And give more than you get. If you do that, you will inevitably get more than you expect.

#giveyourtime

#give2hours

#helpastranger

#helpanybody

"Helping others
is the way we
help ourselves."

–Oprah Winfrey

ABOUT THE AUTHOR

It doesn't matter that Marc Fienberg is an author, movie director, strategy consultant, entrepreneur, owner of The Great Advice Group, husband, and all-around nice guy. What matters is that he is the father of four kids, two of whom are teens. He has served as a life coach to his kids for more than sixteen years, and since none of them have been rushed to the emergency room or spent a night in jail yet, it seems like his Great Advice is working. To learn more about him, go to greatadvicegroup.com.

Made in the USA
Columbia, SC
07 November 2020